Stealing Elections

Stealing Elections

How Voter Fraud Threatens Our Democracy

John Fund

ENCOUNTER BOOKS
NEW YORK · LONDON

Second edition published in 2008 by Encounter Books, an activity of Encounter for Culture and Education, Inc., a nonprofit tax exempt corporation.

Encounter Books website address: www.encounterbooks.com

Cover illustration by David E. Smith, cover design by Jen Huppert.

Manufactured in the United States and printed on acid-free paper.

The paper used in this publication meets the minimum requirements of ANSI/NISO Z39.48-1992 (R 1997) *(Permanence of Paper)*.

ISBN for the second edition: 978-1-59403-224-0

The Library of Congress has cataloged the first edition as follows:

Library of Congress Cataloging-in-Publication Data

Fund, John.
    Stealing elections : how voter fraud threatens our democracy / John Fund.
    p.   cm.
    Includes index.
    ISBN 1-59403-061-8 (alk. paper)
    1. Elections—Corrupt practices—United States.   2. Political corruption
3. United States   I. Title.
JK1994.F86 2004
324.973´0931—dc22

                                                          2004057055

For my family—who taught me to learn about the world without forgetting where I came from.

Contents

Introduction

WITH THE PRESIDENTIAL RACE BETWEEN BARACK Obama and John McCain expected to be very close, our nation may be on the brink of repeating the 2000 Florida election debacle—this time not in one but in several states, with allegations of vote fraud, intimidation and manipulation of voting machines added to the generalized chaos that sent the 2000 race into overtime. There is still time to reduce the chance of another electoral meltdown, both this year and in future years. But this will not happen unless we acknowledge that the United States has a haphazard, fraud-prone election system befitting a developing nation rather than the globe's leading democracy. With its hanging chads, butterfly ballots and Supreme Court interventions at both the state and the federal level, the Florida fiasco compelled this country to confront an ugly reality: that we have been making do with what the noted political scientist Walter Dean Burnham has called "the modern world's sloppiest election systems."

The 2000 Florida recount was more than merely a national embarrassment; it left a lasting scar on the American electoral psyche. A 2004 Zogby poll found that 38 percent of Americans still regard the 2000 election outcome as questionable. Many Republicans believe that Democratic judges on the Florida Supreme Court tried to hand their state to Al Gore based on selective partisan recounts and the illegal votes of felons and aliens. Many Democrats feel that the justices of the U.S. Supreme Court tilted toward Bush, and they refuse to accept his victory as valid. But this issue transcends "red state" vs. "blue state" partisan grievances. Many Americans are convinced that politicians can't be trusted to play by the rules and will either commit fraud or intimidate voters at the slightest opportunity.

A growing cynicism diminishes respect for the nation's institutions and lowers voter participation. Only 11 percent of those eighteen to nineteen years old and eligible to vote for the first time now bother to go to the polls, although there are hopes that Barack Obama's candidacy might change that. Overall, the United States ranks 139th out of 163 democracies in the rate of voter participation. The more that voting is left to the zealous or self-interested few, the more we see harshly personal campaigns that dispense with any positive vision of our national future. "If this escalates, we're in horrendous shape as a country," says Curtis Gans, who runs the Committee for the Study of the American Electorate. "If election results are followed by lawsuits, appeals, fire and counterfire, many people who are already saying to hell with the process are going to exit."

Indeed, the level of suspicion has grown so dramatically that it threatens to undermine our political system. A Rasmussen Reports survey found early in 2008 that when it comes to concern about vote fraud, 17 percent believe that large numbers of legitimate voters are prevented from voting. A slightly larger number, 23 percent, believe that large numbers of ineligible people are allowed to vote.

Those findings were confirmed in a February 2008 survey conducted for the Congressional Cooperative Election Study group, a respected political science organization. It asked respondents how much vote fraud (defined as someone casting more than one ballot or voting if they weren't a U.S. citizen) there was in elections, as well as how much vote theft (defined as having votes stolen or tampered with). A third question was asked about "voter impersonation," where a person claims to be someone else when casting a vote.

Vote fraud is traditionally the type of election irregularity that Republicans focus on, while vote theft is often cited by Democrats worried about manipulation of electronic voting machines. The results were illuminating. A full 62 percent of voters thought vote fraud was very common or somewhat common, versus 28 percent who thought it occurred infrequently or almost never. As for vote theft, 60 percent of respondents thought it was a serious problem, while 29 percent thought it was occasional or rare. Voter impersonation was a much closer question, with 41 percent thinking it happened a great deal or fairly often, and 42 percent thinking it was an unusual occurrence.

Interestingly, Democrats were only slightly more likely than Republicans to state that vote theft is very common, according to an analysis of the poll by Professors Stephen Ansolabehere and Nathaniel Persily. But twice as many Republicans as Democrats thought vote fraud to be very common. As for voter impersonation, Democrats were somewhat skeptical that it was a problem, but among Republicans only 5 percent of respondents thought it was very rare. "Party remains a significant predictor of beliefs about both Fraud and Impersonation in a multivariate analysis that controls for ideology, education, age, race, income and region," concluded the two scholars.

The 2000 election resulted in some modest reforms at the federal level, such as the Help America Vote Act (HAVA) of 2002, but the implementation has been slow. Many of the nation's voting systems will be in no better shape this November than they were in 2000, when about 2 percent of all votes for president nationwide were not counted for one reason or another, the vast majority because of voter error or outdated machines.

America's election problems go beyond the strapped budgets of many local election offices. More insidious are flawed voter rolls, voter ignorance, lackadaisical law enforcement and a shortage of trained volunteers. All this adds up to an open invitation for errors, miscounts or fraud.

Reform is easy to talk about but difficult to bring about. Many of the suggested improvements, such as requiring voters to show ID at the polls, are bitterly opposed. For instance, Maria Cardona of the Democratic National Committee claims that "ballot security and preventing vote fraud are just code words for voter intimidation and suppression." Similarly, many Republicans express great concern for combating voter impersonation through photo ID laws but are less than eager to tackle the loopholes that make absentee ballot fraud a growth industry, because that way of voting is highly popular with middle-class people. Even improved technology is controversial. Some computer scientists are alarmed by the possibility that hackers could change the software in electronic voting machines to cast multiple votes or do other kinds of mischief. Senator Hillary Clinton (Democrat) and Congressman Steve King of Iowa (Republican) have backed separate pieces of legislation to require that voting machines issue paper receipts for voters to verify before casting their ballots.

Confusion and claims of fraud are likely in November 2008, especially if the election is as close as it was in both 2000 and 2004. Can the nation take another controversy of that scale?

Indeed, we may be on the way to turning Election Day into Election Month through a new legal quagmire: election by litigation. Every close race now carries with it the prospect of lawsuits and demands for recounts and seating challenges in Congress. "We are waiting for the day those polls can just cut out the middleman and settle all elections in court," jokes Chuck Todd, the political director of NBC News. Such gallows humor may be entirely appropriate given our current predicament. The 2000 election may have marked a permanent change in how elections are decided, much as the battle over the Supreme Court nomination of Robert Bork changed, apparently forever, the politics of judicial appointments. On April 19, 2004, Senator John Kerry campaigned in Florida and announced—six months before a single ballot was cast, counted or disputed—that he was ready to take the 2004 election to court. "We are going to bring legal challenge to those districts that make it difficult for people to register. We're going to bring challenge to those people that disembroil [*sic*] people," he told a rally. "And we're going to challenge any place in America where you cannot trace the vote and count the votes of Americans. Period!"

Barack Obama has been even more forceful. Last year, he told the *Chicago Defender* that "Recent elections have shown unprecedented intimidation of African American, Native American, low income and elderly voters at the polls. We've seen political operatives purge voters from registration rolls for no legitimate reason, distribute polling equipment unevenly, and deceive voters about the time, location and rules of elections."

Democrats plan to have over ten thousand lawyers on the ground in all states this November, ready for action if the election is close and they see a way to contest it. Republicans will have their own corps of attorneys at the ready. "If you think of election problems as akin to forest fires, the woods are not drier than they were in previous years, but many more people have matches," says Doug Chapin of Electionline.org, an Internet clearinghouse of election news. If the trend toward litigation continues, winners in the future may have to hope not only that they win but that their margins of victory are beyond the "margin of litigation."

"If it's a very close election, we're in real trouble," said Peg Rosenfeld, who has been a prominent official of the League of Women Voters in the battleground state of Ohio for the last forty years. Daniel Okapi, a law professor at Ohio State University, says that weeks of litigation are guaranteed if the winning candidate in the next election has a lead smaller than 5,000 votes. Only a margin of 50,000 votes or more would mean the outcome will probably not be litigated. In 2004, President Bush won the state by only 119,000 votes, and many expect a closer race between Obama and McCain.

Some of the sloppiness that makes fraud and foul-ups in election counts possible seems to be built into the system by design. The National Voter Registration Act ("Motor Voter Law"), the first piece of legislation signed by President Bill Clinton upon entering office in 1993, imposed fraud-friendly rules on the states by requiring driver's license bureaus to register anyone who applies for a license, to offer mail-in registration with no identification needed, and to forbid government workers to challenge new registrants, while making it difficult to purge "deadwood" voters (those who have died or moved away). In 2001, the voter rolls in many American cities included more names than the U.S. Census listed as the total number of residents over age eighteen. CBS's *60 Minutes* created a stir in 1999 when it found people in California using mail-in forms to register fictitious people or actual pets and then obtaining absentee ballots in their names. By this means, for example, the illegal alien who assassinated the Mexican presidential candidate Luis Donaldo Colosio was registered to vote in San Pedro, California—twice. Luckily, some progress has been made in cleaning up those rolls, but many cities are sitting on a sea of invalid registrations that could potentially be converted into votes.

Ironically, Mexico and many other countries have election systems that are far more secure than ours. To obtain voter credentials, the citizen must present a photo, write a signature and give a thumbprint. The voter card includes a picture with a hologram covering it, a magnetic strip and a serial number to guard against tampering. To cast a ballot, voters must present the card and be certified by a thumbprint scanner. This system was instrumental in allowing the 2000 election of Vicente Fox, the first opposition party candidate to be elected president of Mexico in seventy years.

But in the United States, at a time of heightened security and mundane rules that require citizens to show ID to travel and even rent a video, only about half the states require some form of documentation in order to vote. "Why should the important process of voting be the one exception to this rule?" asks Karen Saranita, a former fraud investigator for a Democratic state senator in California. Americans agree. A Rasmussen Reports poll finds that 80 percent of Americans, including three-fourths of Democrats, believe that "people should be required to show a photo identification such as a driver's license before being allowed to vote."

The reason for such support is that citizens instinctively realize that some people will be tempted to cut corners in the cutthroat world of politics. "Some of the world's most clever people are attracted to politics, because that's where the power is," says Larry Sabato, a political scientist at the University of Virginia. "So they're always going to be one step ahead of the law."

Election fraud, whether it's phony voter registrations, illegal absentee ballots, shady recounts or old-fashioned ballot box stuffing, can be found in every part of the United States, although it is probably spreading because of the ever-so-tight divisions that have polarized the country and created so many close elections lately. Although most fraud is found in urban areas, there are current scandals in rural Texas and Minnesota. In recent years, Baltimore, Philadelphia, New Orleans, Seattle and Milwaukee have all had election-related scandals. Wisconsin officials convicted a New York heiress who was working for Al Gore by giving homeless people cigarettes if they rode in a van to the polls and voted.

Then there is the Ford family of Tennessee, which has dominated Memphis politics for a couple of generations and almost elected Harold Ford Jr., the son of a former congressman, to the U.S. Senate in 2006. One burden Ford had in the race was the unsavory record of his family in Memphis elections. Earlier in 2006, the Tennessee State Senate voted to void the election of his aunt Ophelia Ford after it was learned that three poll workers had faked votes in her behalf, including at least two votes cast in the names of dead people.

A few months earlier, Harold Ford Sr., the former congressman and father of the Senate candidate, landed in trouble when it was revealed that he had voted in a Memphis election even though he had taken advantage of a homestead tax break for Florida residents by telling officials there that his $2.5 million home on Miami Beach's Fisher Island was his primary and permanent residence. Casting a ballot in Tennessee while knowing that one is ineligible to vote in that state is a felony. Reached by reporters, Ford was in no mood to talk about the matter. "I'm in a lunch meeting," he said, "and I don't have time." He did not respond to subsequent calls, and the issue faded from public view. But such incidents probably contributed to his son's narrow defeat in the Senate race.

The *Miami Herald* won a Pulitzer Prize for uncovering how "vote brokers" employed by the candidate Xavier Suarez stole a Miami mayoral election in 1997 by tampering with 4,740 absentee ballots. Many were cast by homeless people who didn't live in the city and were paid $10 apiece and shuttled to the election office in vans. All the absentee ballots were thrown out by a court four months later and Mr. Suarez's opponent Joe Carollo was installed as mayor.

But such interventions are rare, even when fraud is proven. In 1997, the House of Representatives voted along partisan lines to demand that the Justice Department prosecute Hermandad Mexicana Nacional, a group that investigators for the House Administration Committee say registered hundreds of illegal voters in a razor-thin congressional race in Orange County, California. But federal immigration officials refused to cooperate with the probe, citing "privacy" concerns, and nothing was done beyond yanking a federal contract that paid Hermandad to conduct citizenship classes. The same year, a U.S. Senate probe into fraud in a Senate election in Louisiana found more than 1,400 cases in which two voters used the same Social Security number. But further investigations collapsed after Democratic senators walked off the probe, calling it unfair, and then Attorney General Janet Reno removed FBI agents from the case because the probe wasn't "bipartisan."

A note about partisanship: Since Democrats figure prominently in the vast majority of examples of election fraud described in this book, some readers will jump to the conclusion that this is a one-sided attack on a single party. I do not believe Republicans are inherently more virtuous or honest than anyone else in politics—far from it. I myself often vote a third-party or independent ticket and have voted for some Democrats.

Vote fraud occurs both in Republican strongholds such as Kentucky hollows and in Democratic bastions such as New Orleans. When Republicans operated political machines such as Philadelphia's Meehan dynasty up until 1951 or the patronage mill of Nassau County, New York, until the 1990s, they were fully capable of bending—and breaking—the rules. The late Earl Mazo, the journalist who exhaustively documented the electoral fraud in Richard J. Daley's Chicago that may have handed Illinois to John F. Kennedy in the photo-finish 1960 election, said there was also "definitely fraud" in downstate Illinois counties controlled by Republicans "but they didn't have the votes to counterbalance Chicago."

While they have not often had the complete control of local and administrative offices that makes it easiest to tilt the rules improperly in their favor, Republicans have at times been guilty of intimidation tactics designed to discourage voting. In the 1980s, the Republican National Committee hired off-duty policemen to monitor polling places in minority areas of New Jersey and Louisiana, until the public outcry forced them to sign a consent decree forswearing all such "ballot security" programs in the future.

In their book *Dirty Little Secrets*, Larry Sabato and Glenn Simpson noted another reason why Republican election fraud is less common: Republican base voters are middle-class and not easily induced to commit fraud, while "the pools of people who appear to be available and more vulnerable to an invitation to participate in vote fraud tend to lean Democratic." Sabato remarks that election fraud tends to be "class-based" because "a poor person has more incentive to sell his vote than an upper class suburbanite."

Those few Democrats who engage in outright dishonesty find it easiest to encourage poor people—who need money—to participate in shady vote-buying schemes. "I had no choice. I was hungry that day," Thomas Felder told the *Miami Herald* in explaining why he illegally voted in the Suarez-Carollo mayoral election. "You wanted the money; you were told who to vote for." Those who buy the votes often have their own kind of hunger. A former Democratic congressman gave me this explanation of why voting irregularities crop up more often in his party's back yard: "When many Republicans lose an election, they go back into what they call the private sector even if it's subsidized at public expense. When many Democrats lose an election, they lose power and money. They need to eat, and people will do an awful lot in order to eat."

Investigation of vote fraud is inherently political, and because it often involves race, it is often not zealously pursued or prosecuted. Attorney General John Ashcroft did launch a Voting Integrity Initiative in 2002, which dramatically reduced both Republican allegations of fraud and Democratic complaints of minority voter suppression. But the program became highly controversial after the 2006 elections when evidence surfaced that the White House had leaned on the Justice Department to replace several U.S. attorneys who had dragged their feet on cases of vote fraud, including David Iglesias in New Mexico and John McKay in Washington State. Even though the firings were perfectly legal, Justice Department lawyers have since then largely retreated from any major role in pursuing cases of vote fraud or voter intimidation.

My research found that the number of people who have actually spent time in jail as a result of a conviction for vote fraud is shockingly low. Most of those who are found guilty get a fine or community service. A vote fraudster in Detroit joked to me that the penalty is often viewed as the cost of doing business. The U.S. attorney for the Northern District of Louisiana, Donald Washington, told a reporter in 2004 that "most of the time, we can't do much of anything [about ballot box improprieties] until the election is over. And the closer we get to the election, the less willing we are to get involved because of just the appearance of impropriety, just the appearance of the federal government somehow signaling how this election ought to occur." Several prosecutors told me they fear charges of racism or of a return to Jim Crow voter-suppression tactics if they pursue fraud cases. Wade Henderson of the Leadership Conference on Civil Rights dismisses efforts to fight election fraud as "a solution in search of a problem" and "a warmed-over plan for voter intimidation."

But when voters are disenfranchised by the counting of improperly cast ballots or outright fraud, their civil rights are violated just as surely as if they were prevented from voting. The integrity of the ballot box is just as important to the credibility of elections as access to it. Voting irregularities have a long pedigree in America stretching back to the founding of the nation—although most people think the "bad old days" ended circa 1948 after pistol-packing Texas sheriffs helped stuff Ballot Box 13, stealing a U.S. Senate seat for Lyndon Johnson. Then came the 2004 Democratic primary election in the same part of Texas, when Representative Ciro Rodriguez, a Democrat, charged that during a recount, a missing ballot box reappeared with enough votes to make his opponent the Democratic candidate by 58 votes. Political bosses such as Richard J. Daley or George Wallace may have died, but they have successors. A one-party machine in Hawaii intimidates critics and journalists who question its vote harvesting among noncitizens. In Alaska, native tribes are often preyed upon by both parties and offered inducements to vote for one candidate or another.

Even after Florida 2000, the media tend to downplay or ignore stories of election incompetence, manipulation or theft. Allowing such abuses to vanish into an informational black hole in effect legitimates them. The refusal to insist on simple procedural changes such as purging voter rolls or requiring a photo ID at the polls, combined with secure technology and more vigorous prosecution of fraud, accelerates our drift toward Banana Republic elections.

In 2002, Miami election officials hired the Center for Democracy, which normally observes voting in places like Guatemala or Albania, to send twenty election monitors to south Florida. Scrutinizing our own elections the way we have traditionally watched over voting in developing countries is, unfortunately, a step in the right direction. But before we can get the clearer laws and better protections we need to deal with fraud and voter mishaps, we have to get a sense of the magnitude of the problem we face.

One

A Conflict of Visions

THE POLLSTER JOHN ZOGBY HAS SPENT A LOT OF TIME analyzing Americans' attitudes toward our election system, particularly in the wake of the bitterly contested 2000 and 2004 presidential votes. The picture his polls draw is one of suspicion and cynicism.

Zogby found that 9 percent of Americans don't believe their votes are counted accurately and another 8 percent aren't sure. Among African Americans, fully 18 percent are skeptical, and among Hispanics the figure is 13 percent. A 2008 Rasmussen Reports poll found that 40 percent of Americans believe there is either significant vote fraud or active suppression of people who want to vote. The percentages are up sharply from November 2000, *after* what was arguably the most contentious vote count in our history, when only 3 percent of those surveyed said they didn't think their vote was counted.

"There is a worrying element of paranoia that is eroding public confidence in the fairness of results," Zogby says. He admits there certainly are lapses in the proper conduct of elections. He recalls doing a study of local election practices for the League of Women Voters in the 1980s and visiting a precinct in his hometown of Utica, New York. After the polls closed at 9:00 P.M., workers spent seven minutes writing down the tallies from the lever machines. "Then one of the workers brought out this big cardboard box filled with absentee ballots," Zogby remembers. "The chief worker said, 'To hell with the absentee ballots. We've been working for fifteen hours straight. Let's go home.' They then called in the final results to the elections office and left."

Many people believe this kind of thing still happens on a regular basis and often in a calculated fashion, but many commentators seem intent on pooh-poohing these fears. "Just as a sizable fraction of American children firmly believe in a bogeyman in the closet, many American adults are gripped by the paranoid fear that the opposing political party regularly steals votes," sneers Dahlia Lithwick, a liberal legal analyst. She disparages the six Supreme Court justices who upheld a landmark voter ID law in 2008 in part because they worried about declining voter confidence in elections. "Voter confidence went wobbly only after partisans started peddling a fictional epidemic in the first place," she claims.

But Mississippi's secretary of state, Delbert Hosemann (a Republican), sees things differently. In pushing for a voter ID bill in his state, he says public officials would be foolish to ignore polls that show 85 percent of people believe vote fraud was key in the last state election. "That's unacceptable that people don't believe you got elected fairly," he told the *Hattiesburg American*. He thinks vote fraud correlates directly with high unemployment and bad schools in certain areas of his state. "We found a woman with throat cancer who sold her vote for $25. We found an unemployed man who sold his vote for a case of beer," he said. "Voter fraud is about keeping the poor people poor."

It's clear that Americans are separated not just by political disagreements but by a basic difference in how we see voting. Democrats gravitate to the view that the most important value is empowering people to exercise their democratic rights, and they worry about people being denied that right. The

Democratic National Committee's Voting Rights Institute emphasizes the need "to remove every barrier that impedes or denies an eligible vote." High in the Democratic Party's pantheon of heroes (far more than they were forty years ago when the party had many segregationist leaders) are "activists from all over America who converged on Mississippi in the summer of 1964 to help educate and register tens of thousands of previously disenfranchised American citizens."

Republicans tend to pay more attention to the rule of law and the standards and procedures that govern elections. Conservative legal scholars have noted that voters as well as election officials have an obligation to make sure that democracy works. Republicans worry publicly about the upcoming presidential election, but not for the same reason as Democrats. "Illegal aliens, homeless people and vote brokers who bus people from place to polling place will all figure in this election," said Rush Limbaugh on his national radio show. Republicans have their own legal team to combat fake voter registrations, absentee ballot fraud and residents of nursing homes being "assisted" in casting votes. The former House majority leader Tom DeLay has been openly dismissive of Democratic claims to want clean elections: "It's their stock in trade to say one thing, and while you're not looking do something shady with the ballots and then cry racism if anyone complains."

On the other side of the aisle, Terry McAuliffe, former DNC chairman, says that while his party "opposes any fraudulent behavior or activity at polling places," the real issue is having the Justice Department ensure that no voter is harassed or intimidated. In 2004, he rejected GOP calls for a joint bipartisan task force that would pair a Republican and a Democratic volunteer to visit problem precincts, saying it was merely a "public relations gambit."

Some Democratic Party allies have had even harsher things to say about Republican efforts to police the polls. Wade

Henderson of the Leadership Conference on Civil Rights contends that such actions "serve no useful purpose other than to prevent people from voting" and that the Justice Department's antifraud efforts under President Bush are really a strategy to scare voters from the polls. Liberal legal groups are suing to set aside laws in some of the states that aim to tighten antifraud protections.

Clearly the nature and conduct of our elections have become a highly polarized political issue. Getting the parties to agree on anything in the heat of a rancorous election season is well-nigh impossible. Al Gore's decision to contest the 2000 election in Florida until the bitter end may have permanently changed the way close elections are handled. The Bush administration's ham-handed replacement of two or more U.S. attorneys in 2006 for failing to prosecute vote fraud cases has tainted the Justice Department's reputation for nonpartisan enforcement of election laws in the eyes of many people. If the 2008 election and future contests are close, the doubts that have collected around the way we vote (and count our votes) could guarantee endless lawsuits and recriminations that will poison public opinion and create a climate of illegitimacy around any final winner.

A Clash of Worldviews

In his classic 1988 book *A Conflict of Visions: The Ideological Origins of Political Struggles*, the economist Thomas Sowell outlined the important role that social "visions" play in our thinking. By "vision" he meant a fundamental sense of how the world works.

For decades, public opinion researchers sought the perfect polling question that best correlated with whether someone considered himself a Republican or a Democrat. In the 1960s, Gallup finally came up with the question that has had the most consistent predictive power over the last forty years: "In your opinion, which is more often to blame if a person is poor? Lack of effort on his own part, or circumstances beyond his control?" Today, as might be expected of a divided nation, these two competing views on what creates poverty are equally strong in their hold on American public opinion.

Competing visions or worldviews are particularly powerful in determining how people think about issues because, unlike "class interests" or other motivating forces, they are largely invisible, even—or especially—to those who harbor them. They explain how so often in life the same people continually line up on the same sides of different issues. Sowell maintains that conflicts of visions dominate history. "We will do almost anything for our visions, except think about them," he concludes. Sowell identifies two distinct visions that shape the debate on controversial issues. The first he calls the "unconstrained" vision of human nature and the second he terms the "constrained" vision.

Those with an unconstrained vision think that if we want a society where people are enlightened, prosperous and equal, we must develop programs to accomplish those goals and work to implement them. The focus is on results or outcomes. That would include making sure as many people as possible vote, thus animating the ideals of democracy.

Sometimes the desire to expand voting opportunities takes on unrealistic qualities. Before he became New York's governor, David Paterson sponsored a bill to allow noncitizen residents to vote in local elections. He now has backed off "active" support of that idea. But the San Francisco Board of Supervisors placed a measure on the ballot in 2004 that would have allowed noncitizens to vote in school board races. "Candidates who run for school board ought to have to campaign in immigrant communities that are filling the public schools with kids," maintained Matt Gonzalez, a supervisor who was the proposal's chief sponsor. But the city attorney, Louise Renne (a Democrat), was no less adamant that state law bars noncitizens from voting. "What's next? Osama bin Laden voting?" she asked. Even San Francisco voters found the proposal too much and voted it down.

Those with a "constrained" vision of human nature, on the other hand, believe that the goal of reason should be not to remodel society, but rather to identify "natural laws" and work within them. Such people focus on general rules and processes. In the area of elections, the constrained vision would favor setting up procedures to make certain that votes are counted accurately and fairly, but not bending these procedures to increase voter participation.

During the 2000 Florida recount I came across many people who represented each of these conflicting visions. At a Jesse Jackson rally I attended, the crowd chanted "Count Every Vote!" and "One Ballot Is One Vote." Meanwhile, many Republicans I met carried a brochure from the Florida Department of Law Enforcement that outlined "Voter Responsibilities." It read in part:

> Each registered voter in this state should:
>
> Familiarize himself or herself with the candidates and issues.
>
> Maintain with the supervisor of elections a current address. Know the location of his or her polling place and its hours. Bring proper identification to the polls. Familiarize himself or herself with the voting equipment in his or her precinct.
>
> Make sure that his or her completed ballot is correct.

"I run into two kinds of people," says Mischelle Townsend, the former registrar of Riverside County, California. "The first is focused on making sure everything is geared to increasing turnout and making sure no one is disenfranchised. The other is more interested in making sure things get done right, are secure and the law is followed." She vividly recalls the

2003 recall that put Arnold Schwarzenegger in office as governor of California. The ACLU, the NAACP and other liberal groups convinced a three-judge panel of the U.S. Court of Appeals for the Ninth Circuit to cancel the election because six counties still used punch-card ballots, which according to the anti-recall plaintiffs had a higher error rate than other forms of voting. The argument was that some minority voters would thus be disenfranchised. But an eleven-member panel of the Ninth Circuit unanimously rejected that view, contending that postponing a recall election was tantamount to disenfranchising all voters.

According to the pollster Scott Rasmussen, significantly more Democrats than Republicans today are convinced that elections are not fair. But this is partly the vision of people out of power. "During the Clinton years my surveys showed more Democrats thought elections were fair to voters, while Republicans were less convinced," he says. "I guess attitudes depend in part on whether your side won or not."

Regardless of how the views of some people might shift, whoever holds extreme versions of either vision isn't helping our election system. An excessively cramped view of elections, holding that rules and procedures must be interpreted in such a way as to guarantee that absolutely no improper vote is cast, may be regarded as unfairly denying some people the right to vote. Antifraud efforts that cross the line, such as stationing off-duty cops at polling places as some Republican campaigns did in the 1980s, invite a response such as that of Steven Hill, a senior analyst for the Center for Voting and Democracy: "There must be something about certain types of voters that Republicans don't trust."

At the other extreme, a loose and lax approach toward the law can lead to unacceptable attempts to game the system, such as the one that created thousands of suspect voter registrations during South Dakota's photo-finish Senate race in

2002. Maka Duta, the woman at the heart of that scandal, admitted duplicating signatures on both registration forms and applications for absentee ballots. But she asked for understanding: "If I erred in doing so, I pray that Attorney General Barnett will agree with me that I erred on the side of angels." In other words, doing the devil's work of forging voter signatures is somehow understandable given her angelic goal of increasing voter turnout.

Despite the passionate opinions on each side as to what undermines the electoral process, there are potential points of agreement that both "visions" should be able to see with clarity. Donna Brazile, who served as Al Gore's campaign manager in 2000, shares his outrage over the Florida outcome. But she also says, "Both parties should want every voter having information and training to cast a ballot that counts. And if that's done, both parties should support steps to ensure every vote cast is a valid and proper one."

Mary Kiffmeyer, a Republican who was chairman of the National Association of Secretaries of State from 2005 to 2006, also endorses having both government and political parties do more to make sure that voters understand how to vote and what is involved. Both women agree that high school curricula, which now often teach students what to eat, how to balance a checkbook and other mundane tasks, should also include instruction on voting. Many high schools invite seniors to volunteer to work at polling places on Election Day; they earn academic credit in their civics classes as well as a small stipend for the day's work.

Still, everyone knows it will be some time before voter education contributes to a reduction in tension between those who hold so firmly their competing visions of what's important in an election. Meanwhile, we have national elections taking place every two years in an atmosphere of mistrust and bitter division that makes governance increasingly difficult.

The Bloody Eighth

There has been much speculation about when and how the current era of political hard feelings between the two parties—usually described by the catchall term "polarization"—began. Some trace it to the Iran-Contra scandal of 1986; some say the nomination of Robert Bork the next year; some pick the Clarence Thomas confirmation fight in 1991. Others say it stemmed from the intense, almost visceral reaction many people had to Bill Clinton, culminating in his 1998 impeachment. Whichever event was most influential, the tone of debate in politics has gradually grown more acrimonious, personal and cynical over the last two decades.

But the U.S. Congress has never had a more bitterly partisan battle—or one that more plainly displayed the clash of competing visions over vote counting—than it did in early 1984, when it had to decide the razor-thin election in Indiana's Eighth Congressional District, known locally as the "Bloody Eighth" for its many close contests.

Voting on Election Day 1984 showed the Democratic incumbent Frank McCloskey with a 72-vote victory. His Republican opponent, Rick McIntyre, then filed for a partial recount (anticipating Al Gore's 2000 attempt to cherry-pick favorable counties in Florida), and McCloskey counterfiled for a district-wide recount. The recount deteriorated into full-scale chaos after some 5,000 ballots, cast mostly it was said by black voters, were tossed out in Evansville because of mistakes by poll clerks. When the counting was done, McIntyre held a 418-vote lead and he was certified the winner by the Republican secretary of state.

When McIntyre came to Washington to be sworn in as a member of Congress, Democrats had him stand to the side when other members took the oath of office. Then they voted to keep the seat vacant pending an investigation of the contest.

The House Administration Committee appointed a three-member task force to oversee a General Accounting Office recount of all the ballots, while both men drew a congressional salary but had no job.

During the recount, Republicans tried several times to seat McIntyre but were defeated on party-line votes. Finally, the task force voted two to one, also on party lines, to declare McCloskey the winner by four votes. GOP protests went unheeded and Republican members walked out of the chamber after the House vote seated McCloskey.

The subject remains a sensitive one with many House members even today. "It was the event that stimulated the Republican revolution and breakdown of amicable relations between the parties," says David Keene, president of the American Conservative Union. "Every Republican believes that election was stolen during the final recount."

Republican Strong-Arm Tactics

Democrats say that Indiana Republicans got their revenge for the McCloskey-McIntyre race a decade later, in 1995. After a recount in a state senate race in Lake County, Indiana, the incumbent Democratic state senator, Frank Mrvan Jr., was three votes behind his Republican challenger, Sandra Dempsey. But election workers at three precincts realized they had misfiled some absentee ballots, most of them from Mrvan neighborhoods.

Indiana law stated that in cases of error by an election official, voter intent should prevail. When the issue came up before the state senate, however, the Republican majority ruled that the ballots had been "tainted" and could not be counted. The Republicans booted Mrvan from office and swore in Dempsey. The conservative *Indianapolis News* called the move "pure, unadulterated self-serving partisanship." But

Mrvan had the last laugh, coming back to reclaim the seat by defeating Dempsey in 1996.

Despite strong-arm tactics like this, many Republicans are convinced that their party has a monopoly on virtue when it comes to the devious art of election theft. They don't. Anyone who spent time in the 1990s around nicotine-stained GOP party hacks in Nassau County, where lucrative patronage jobs were considered a form of gold and winning elections an easy way to mine for such jobs, would laugh at the suggestion.

During 2007, the new Democratic Congress made much of the news that several U.S. attorneys were harshly criticized for not bringing corruption or vote fraud cases against Democrats. Two were ultimately replaced in part for their failure to pursue what some in Justice thought were obvious cases of wrongdoing.

One of the dismissed federal prosecutors was David Iglesias, the U.S. attorney in New Mexico, who claims that he tried to find a vote fraud case but couldn't come up with anything solid. In his new book, which slams the Bush Justice Department for being overly political, Iglesias claims that he now views alleged voter-suppression tactics as a more serious problem. He cites the practice of "vote caging," which he described to the columnist Amy Goodman as "when you send voter information to a group of people that you have reason to believe are no longer there, such as military personnel who are overseas, such as students at historically black colleges. When it comes back as undeliverable, the party uses that information to remove that person from the voter rolls, claiming they are no longer there. It is a reprehensible practice." Iglesias hopes that in 2008 "the Democratic Party and the media really keep a lot of pressure on this."

Republicans have certainly at times stepped way over the line in trying to root out vote fraud in minority communities. In the 1990s, the North Carolina Republican Party mailed postcards to hundreds of thousands of black voters telling them they would go to prison if they voted improperly. In 1988, California Republicans in one assembly district hired guards in blue uniforms at twenty polling places. They stood holding signs in Spanish and English that read "Noncitizens can't vote." Republicans later settled a lawsuit over the issue for some $400,000, admitting to no wrongdoing. During the New Jersey governor's race in 1981, Republicans stationed armed guards wearing black armbands in front of largely minority polling places. The Republican candidate, Tom Kean Sr., wound up winning by 1,797 votes. The subsequent civil lawsuit was settled for one dollar.

An even more publicized incident involving an effort to suppress minority voter turnout occurred in 1986 when the Republican National Committee agreed to end a ballot security program in Louisiana. It had sent letters to voters in precincts where the GOP had gotten less than 20 percent of the vote in 1984 to see if they actually lived at the address shown on their registrations. If the letters were returned by the post office—as 31,000 were—the names were handed over to voter registrars with a request that they be purged. A judge found that the precincts where GOP support was below 20 percent coincided almost exactly with precincts where blacks were a clear majority, and he ruled that the program had singled out minorities.

Democrats sued in federal court. During discovery, they found an e-mail sent before the 1986 election by an RNC official to the party's southern political director. The key passage read: "I would guess that this program will eliminate at least 60,000 to 80,000 folks from the rolls. If it's a close race, which I'm assuming it is, this could keep the black vote down considerably." Clearly, Republicans had erred in not sending letters to all households in the state when they sought to purge the voter rolls. They agreed not to conduct such programs in the future. Since then, the national GOP has been terminally gun-shy of launching any program that could be characterized as trying to prevent minorities from voting, but the perception that they are doing so lingers.

Democrats frequently make hay by charging that Republi-cans are bringing back the ghost of Jim Crow to block minor-ity participation. In her 2000 Senate race, Hillary Clinton ended her campaign with a Brooklyn College rally filled with Haitian Americans. She told them of a GOP "plot" to put off-duty police officers and prison guards at targeted polling places to intimidate voters. "I urge you to be vigilant," she shouted. All that was missing was a reference to "the vast vote-suppression conspiracy." No evidence of such a program has ever been found.

Yet some Republican dirty tricks are the real thing. In 2004, the Justice Department threw the book at the former president of a Virginia-based telemarketing firm who tried to jam Democratic get-out-the-vote phone lines in the 2002 election in New Hampshire. Allen Raymond was sent to prison for taking $15,600 from the state GOP office for get-out-the-vote calls for its candidates and then using $2,500 of the money to have another company repeatedly call five phone lines at Democratic offices. "We shut down the Democratic Party's election-day phone bank so no phone calls could go in or out. That was a dirty trick and a crime, and I was punished," Raymond acknowledged.

The phone-jamming scheme resulted in three criminal prosecutions and a lawsuit that forced Republicans to pay Democrats $135,000. Charles McGee, former executive direc-tor of the New Hampshire Republican Party, pleaded guilty and served seven months in prison for his role. James Tobin, former regional director for the Republican National Com-mittee, was convicted of helping arrange the phone jam, but he was later acquitted on all charges on appeal.

The most amusing example of GOP election fraud occurred in wild and wooly Las Vegas, the fastest-growing city in America. In April 2003, Gary and Pamela Horrocks were indicted on charges that they had asked several people who patronized the tavern they owned to fill out bogus voter registration cards and requests for absentee ballots. The previous year, Gary Horrocks had lost a GOP primary for a state assembly seat to a twenty-five-year-old newcomer, Francis Allen. Horrocks had contempt for Allen and announced publicly that he would submarine her chances in the 2002 general election race against Marcus Conklin, a Democrat. But no one expected him to go as far as he did, or to boast about it.

On election night of 2002, just after it became clear that Francis Allen had lost the race by 134 votes, Horrocks showed up at an election party held at Caesars Palace and walked up to Francis Deane, the elected county recorder. "He related to me that he had obtained over a hundred absentee votes in the election for me," Deane recalled. When she asked him how he knew this, he revealed that he had absentee ballots mailed to himself and his wife and they filled them out; he therefore knew how many votes he was responsible for. Indeed, Horrocks told her that he was late to the event that night because he had just delivered three votes. Deane still shakes her head at how his scheme was uncovered only because the perpetrator opened his big mouth. "He was so proud. He was like the cat that ate the canary."

Horrocks was less happy once investigators fanned out and discovered that 160 voters had illegally registered to vote in the race that Allen lost and had their absentee ballots mailed either to Horrocks' tavern or to another mailbox that he controlled. Horrocks claimed he had been misunderstood by Deane. The prosecutors responded that he had been heard perfectly and the evidence backed up his boast.

But even this open-and-shut case moved with agonizing slowness, as the *Las Vegas Review-Journal* noted. "It wasn't clear whether anyone at the district attorney's office or the Clark County Election Department wanted to do anything about it. Southern Nevada has a long history of shady campaign activity, but a remarkably brief record of actually prosecuting the corruption." Finally, in early 2008—over five years after the fraud was uncovered—Horrocks and his wife were fined $7,000, put on probation and sentenced to community service. Once again, even a blatant self-confessed vote stealer didn't serve even a single day in jail for his crime. The lesson other fraudsters would take is that it takes a lot to be prosecuted for vote fraud, and the penalty isn't very onerous. And don't think the Horrocks case was an aberration. The *Review-Journal* remarked that it merely offered "a glimpse of Southern Nevada's seamy underbelly" in elections.

Indeed, Las Vegas papers in 2004 were again filled with stories on election fraud. Larry Lomax, Clark County's top election official, announced that he had uncovered a surge in phony registrations. "We've never seen anything close to this," he warned. He believed that many of the phony registrations flooding his office had escaped detection. "There are stupid criminals out there, and there are smart ones," Lomax said. "We can spot the stupid ones because they submit them in a stack." But he wasn't sure if anyone would ever uncover the more devious fraud.

Democrats' Motor Voters

Perhaps no piece of legislation in the last generation better captures the "incentivizing" of fraud and the clash of conflicting visions about the priorities of our election system than the 1993 National Voter Registration Act, commonly known as the "Motor Voter Law." Observers always regarded the timing of the push for Motor Voter as curious. It was the first major legislative priority for the new Clinton White House, even though it had just won an election in which the country had seen the largest increase in voter turnout in a generation. Nonetheless, President Clinton declared a "crisis" in civic participation and proceeded to ram the proposed law through Congress.

The law imposed an unfunded mandate on the states by requiring that anyone entering a government office to renew a driver's license or apply for welfare or unemployment compensation would be offered the chance to register on the spot to vote. Examiners were under orders not to ask anyone for identification or proof of citizenship. States also had to permit mail-in voter registration, which allowed anyone to register without any personal contact with a registrar or election official. Finally, states were limited in clearing their rolls of "deadwood"—people who had died or moved or been convicted of crimes. Now, people who didn't vote would be kept on the rolls for at least eight years before anyone could remove them.

Since its implementation, Motor Voter has worked in one sense: it has fueled an explosion of phantom voters. Between 1994 and 1998, nearly 26 million names were added to the voter rolls nationwide, almost a 20 percent increase. Ironically, as the bipartisan polling team of Ed Goeas and Celinda Lake points out, perhaps only 5 percent of those who register when they get a driver's license routinely vote, so the policy has artificially driven down voter turnout percentages and led to yet more cries that something be done about the "turnout crisis."

Curtis Gans, director of the Committee for the Study of the American Electorate, supports some form of national voter registration, but says voter lists from around the country are in pathetic shape—even with the statewide databases created after Congress passed the Help America Vote Act (HAVA) in 2002. Gans believes that the deadwood clogging our voter rolls provides the unscrupulous with opportunities to vote in the name of someone they can safely predict will not show up at the polls to challenge them.

This assumption was supported by a 2000 investigation by the *Indianapolis Star*'s Bill Theobald, who reported that "hundreds of thousands of names, as many as one in five statewide," were on Indiana registration rolls improperly "because the people behind those names have moved, died or gone to prison." Mark Kruzan, the Democratic floor leader in the Indiana House of Representatives at the time, commented, "It has become almost ridiculous. I don't know if there is fraud, but it invites the possibility of fraud." Kruzan tried to pass a law to purge the rolls of invalid names, but in vain.

The sad state of Indiana's voter rolls ultimately led a Republican legislature to pass a law mandating that voters show photo ID. This was the case that went before the Supreme Court in 2008, resulting in such laws being declared constitutional.

Some registration scandals have been comic. In Broward County, Florida, for example, an eight-year-old girl registered to vote. The error would not have been caught if the girl hadn't been summoned for jury duty, whereupon her mother called officials to report the mistake. Less amusing is the accumulating evidence that Motor Voter has been registering illegal aliens, since anyone who receives a government benefit may also register to vote with no questions asked. A federal immigration probe in 1996 into alleged Motor Voter fraud in California's Orange County revealed that "4,023 illegal voters possibly cast ballots in the disputed election between Robert Dornan and Loretta Sanchez" for Congress. Dornan lost that race by fewer than 1,000 votes.

But cries for reform have been stymied when the inevitable "race card' is played. In 1998, when House Republicans proposed to verify the citizenship of potential registrants, Representative Luis Gutierrez of Illinois accused them of "creating unwarranted fear of the Hispanic community in the eyes of our fellow Americans." Then House Speaker Newt Gingrich responded by saying, "How can we cancel out an American citizen and not feel that we are somehow cheating the essence of freedom in America? This bill is about citizenship. It is about citizens being allowed to vote."

The lax standards for registration encouraged by the Motor Voter law have left the rolls in a shambles in many states. The uncertainty surrounding them breeds mistrust and may call the integrity of the entire system into doubt. Motor Voter has led to an "appearance of corruption" that has, fairly or not, done real damage to American government. In addition, the artificial inflation of the registration rolls has also clearly misled Americans about the state of their democracy by giving a false measure of voter turnout as a percentage of registered voters. Rather than a decline, we may have seen an increase in voting as a percentage of legitimately registered voters; but because of Motor Voter, we just don't know.

For He's a Jolly Good Felon

Hillary Clinton left nothing to chance in preparing to run for president. She realized that the country lacks a natural Democratic majority—no Democrat since Lyndon Johnson in 1964 has won more than 50.1 percent of the popular vote—so it might be necessary, in paraphrase of Bertolt Brecht, to change the electorate. That may explain why in 2005 she moved front and center as lead sponsor of the Count Every Vote Act, which she says is designed to boost voter participation in future elections—including the one in 2008 in which she hoped to be running for president as the Democratic nominee.

The columnist George Will says that Senator Clinton's bill might more aptly be termed the What's a Little Fraud among Friends? Act. After a nod to making Election Day a national holiday—which might do little more than create a de facto Saturday-to-Tuesday four-day weekend—she got down to the real business. The bill made a mockery of the Constitution's stipulation that the states shall determine "the Times, Places and Manner of holding Elections." Instead, all states would be dragooned into following new federal standards on mandatory recounts, provisional ballots, and even voter waiting times. Every state would be compelled to offer no-excuse absentee voting as well as Election Day registration.

Those changes would be open invitations to fraud. Voters recognize as much. They are especially leery of same-day registration; in 2002, electorates in both California and Colorado turned the idea down by three-to-two margins. But the meat of the bill is Clinton's insistence that every state restore voting rights to all convicted criminals "who have repaid their debt to society" by completing their prison terms, parole or probation. She disingenuously refers to them as ex-felons, which is incorrect since the law holds that once someone becomes a felon, he remains one.

The Count Every Vote Act was a breathtaking assertion of federal authority, since the Fourteenth Amendment specifically permits states to disenfranchise citizens convicted of "participation in rebellion, or other crime." But the barriers aren't high in most states, and standards vary greatly. Maine and Vermont let jailbirds vote from their prison cells. A total of thirty-four states and the District of Columbia automatically allow felons who have served their time in prison to vote. Florida and thirteen other states require them to petition to have their voting rights restored. Senator Clinton estimates there are now five million disenfranchised felons in the country, or one out of every forty-four adults.

Most people found it hard to escape the partisan implications of Clinton's move toward felon voting. In a 2003 study, the sociologists Christopher Uggen and Jeff Manza found that roughly a third of disenfranchised felons had completed their prison time or parole and would thus have their vote restored under her bill. An overwhelming majority of felons lean toward one political party—the Democrats. Uggen and Manza estimated that Bill Clinton won 86 percent of the felon vote in the 1992 presidential race and a whopping 93 percent four years later. Voting participation by all felons, they concluded, would have allowed Democrats to win a series of key U.S. Senate elections, thus allowing the party to control the Senate continuously from 1986 until at least this January.

There is some evidence that felons already swing elections even in states where many of them are barred from voting. The *Seattle Times* found that 129 felons in just two counties, King and Pierce, voted illegally in the photo-finish race for governor in Washington State last November. Since the Democratic candidate, Christine Gregoire, won by (coincidentally) 129 votes in the final recount, it appears that she owes her election in part to the felon vote.

The most persistent argument against laws barring felons from voting is that they have their origins in Jim Crow laws passed after the Civil War to prevent blacks from voting. But Alexander Keyssar, a Harvard historian and author of the classic book *The Right to Vote*, points out that many states passed such laws before the Civil War. Later, the laws were passed in many Southern states by Reconstruction governments run by Republicans who supported black voting rights. Keyssar says that "most laws that disenfranchised felons had complex and murky origins," often centering on the notion that "a voter ought to be a moral person." As one judge noted, "Felons are not disenfranchised based on any immutable characteristic, such as race, but on their conscious decision to commit an act for which they assume the risks of detection and punishment."

That notion of individual responsibility, however, is dismissed by liberal academics who sound as if they just stepped off the Berkeley campus of the University of California circa 1965. Elizabeth Hull, a professor at Rutgers University, calls the argument that people are responsible for their own behavior "flawed" because "it rids the community at large of any responsibility for the criminal's behavior, and discounts entirely any contribution poverty or racism or inferior educational institutions or drug-ridden neighborhoods might play in fostering antisocial behavior." Manza and Uggen don't go that far, but they do argue that ending the laws against felon voting might have a positive effect on society. "We don't know whether voting causes reduced crime, but we find a strong correlation," they write. "In our Minnesota data, voters in 1996 were about half as likely to be rearrested from 1997–2000 as non-voters." Of course, extrapolating from Minnesota is a chancy proposition. If all of America were like Minnesota, we'd be a giant Scandinavia. Clearly, much of the country isn't.

Hillary Clinton must have known how much her association with the wacky pro-felon voting community worked against her effort to appear a thoughtful moderate. She apparently calculated that the embarrassment of having people make jibes about her wanting to make Democrats the "Jailbird Party" was small compared with the potential political payoff.

Two

Voters without Borders

THIS YEAR, MORE VOTERS THAN EVER WILL CAST BALLOTS early. The result may be that we get the final election results late. It's possible we won't know which party controls the White House for days or even weeks because of all the disputes and delays caused by absentee ballots.

Thirty states now allow anybody to cast an absentee ballot without having to give an excuse for missing Election Day. That's up from twenty states just six years ago. Several other states also allow early voting at government buildings or even grocery stores. This year, it's expected that three out of ten Americans will vote before Election Day. Many will vote three weeks before the election, and in Maine people can begin voting an astounding *three months* before Election Day.

In states such as Washington, California and Arizona, more than half the ballots are likely to be absentee. In California, more than one in five voters have signed up to receive absentee ballots for every election. Oregon has gone even further: in 2000 it abolished polling places, and now everyone votes by mail.

If control of the White House hinges on a few close states, don't expect to know the final outcome on election night. While early votes cast on electronic machines are easily integrated into the totals from traditional polling places, paper absentee ballots are typically counted only after the others. In

Florida, Pennsylvania and some other states, ballots will still be coming in for days because they are legal if postmarked on or before Election Day. Provisional votes, which are cast when a voter doesn't show up on registration rolls, can also slow down the process. Generally, officials have up to fourteen days to determine if a vote is valid. In 2006, Maryland officials barely met that deadline after snafus with electronic voting machines dramatically increased the number of provisional votes cast in its primary.

In some supertight races, a flood of absentee ballots could delay the results for weeks. "Anytime you have more paper ballots cast outside polling places, the more mistakes and delays you're likely to have," Bill Gardner, New Hampshire's Democratic secretary of state, told me.

Mistakes are certainly possible. In 2004, a worker at an election office in Toledo, Ohio, found three hundred completed absentee ballots in a storage room more than a month after the vote. At least half hadn't been counted, and they affected the result of at least one local contest. In Washington State, absentee ballots were the main reason that two recent statewide contests, for Senate in 2000 and for governor in 2004, went into overtime. "Washington State has regressed in being able to declare a winner since absentee voting now makes up a majority of votes," says John Carlson, a Seattle talk-show host. In 2000, Maria Cantwell (Democrat) had to wait weeks to learn she had squeaked out a 2,200-vote plurality at a time when control of the U.S. Senate was in doubt. "Can anyone say it was a good thing the country had to wait until December 1 to learn the U.S. Senate would be tied?" asks Carlson.

People in our increasingly mobile and hectic society now expect to vote with the same ease and convenience as they buy an airline ticket. But perhaps we should listen to what cautionary voices are telling us before we redefine ourselves as a nation of convenience voters and abandon one of the only remaining occasions on which Americans come together as a nation to perform a collective civic duty.

In the days when Norman Rockwell used to paint *Saturday Evening Post* covers showing people lining up outside churches and schools to vote, it was thought that we all should vote together, and that absentee voting was somehow shirking a voter's true duty and should only be a last resort. In our instant-gratification era, that notion now seems a bit quaint.

But a common voting time was also dictated by the Constitution. Article II states that "Congress may determine the Time of choosing the Election, and the Day on which they shall give their votes, which day shall be the same throughout the United States." Congress codified this requirement in 1872 when it stipulated that presidential elections should be held on the same day throughout the nation. Courts have nonetheless been understandably reluctant to invalidate state laws that go against this dictate.

In 2000, the Voting Integrity Project (VIP) challenged Oregon's radical decision to adopt a completely vote-by-mail system, which 57 percent of state voters had approved in an initiative in 1996. Miller Baker, a lawyer for VIP, said the law made a mockery of the federal statute because ballots could be returned up to three weeks before Election Day. "Absentee voting for good reasons is one thing," he told the court. "But Oregon abolishing voting in person is the difference between the exception to the rule and the exception that swallows the rule." He pointed out that the Oregon system had contributed to the chaos of the 2000 presidential election because final mail-in balloting results—showing that Al Gore had won the state by fewer than seven thousand votes—weren't known for weeks.

But U.S. district judge Ann Aiken disagreed. If the Voting Integrity Project was correct, she ruled, "all state absentee balloting laws would be preempted by federal law." In 2002, a three-judge panel of the U.S. Court of Appeals for the Ninth Circuit affirmed the lower court decision. The judges noted the "considerable force" of VIP's argument, but were convinced that ruling in its favor would endanger absentee balloting for the elderly and disabled. "How can we not at the same time throw out the absentee ballot baby with the bath water?" asked Judge Ruggero J. Aldisert. The panel upheld the vote-by-mail plan because of "a long history of Congressional tolerance" toward absentee voting, particularly in cases where it improves voter turnout.

In fact, however, early and absentee voting may not have boosted turnout. Curtis Gans, the director of the Committee for the Study of the American Electorate, says that "academic studies all show that easy absentee voting decreases or has no effect on turnout," with the 2004 election a slight exception. This is because "you are diffusing the mobilizing focus away from a single day and having to mobilize voters over a period of time." He compares it to the impact a candidate makes on voters when he spends $1 million over the twenty-one-day interval that many states allow for absentee voting, versus the same amount of money focused on a single Election Day. Gans notes that the people who really are helped by absentee voting are those who cast ballots anyway, often "lazy, middle-class and upper-middle-class people."

Voting before the fact also allows voters to cast their ballots before they might receive useful information or telling insights into candidates. Ross Perot suffered his meltdown on *60 Minutes*, in which he accused Republicans of disrupting his daughter's wedding, only nine days before Election Day in 1992. That same year, the independent counsel Lawrence Walsh indicted Caspar Weinberger and other figures in the Iran-Contra scandal only four days before Election Day. The John Huang campaign fundraising scandal accelerated in the days just prior to the 1996 election. Elizabeth Drew quotes Bill Clinton as admitting that the Huang scandal prevented the Democrats from regaining control of the House. Jeff Jacoby, a *Boston Globe* columnist, says that having so many people vote weeks early "is rather like having a judge announce that any juror may vote and go home" when the juror decides he or she has heard enough evidence.

It's certainly true that voters like no-excuses absentee voting for its convenience. "Forcing voters to go to the polls to cast their ballots is an antiquated, outdated, absurd practice," says Oren Spiegler, a Pennsylvania voter. But convenience comes at a price. Simply put, absentee voting makes it easier to commit election fraud, because the ballots are cast outside the supervision of election officials. "By loosening up the restrictions on absentee voting they have opened up more chances for fraud," Damon Stone, a former election fraud investigator in West Virginia, told the *New York Times*.

"The lack of in-person, at-the-polls accountability makes absentee ballots the tool of choice for those inclined to commit fraud," the Florida Department of Law Enforcement concluded in 1998, after a mayoral election in Miami was thrown out when it was learned that "vote brokers" had signed hundreds of phony absentee ballots. It was after this scandal that Florida tightened its absentee ballot laws—changes that proved very helpful to Gore during the recount.

It's so easy to cheat with absentees, you'd be surprised who's been caught at it. In 1998, a former Democratic congressman from Pennsylvania, Austin Murphy, was convicted of absentee ballot fraud in a nursing home, where residents' failing mental capacities make them an easy mark. "In this area there's a pattern of nursing home administrators frequently forging ballots under residents' names," Sean Cavanagh, a former Democratic county supervisor from the area, told me. He says that many nursing home owners rely on regular "bounties" from candidates whom they allow to enter their facilities and harvest votes.

Toby Moffett, a former Democratic congressman, can attest to the last-minute surprises that absentees create. In the late 1980s, he won the Democratic primary race for governor of Connecticut on the day of the primary, but ended up losing by 43 votes after absentees were counted. Several of his opponent's supporters were later arrested for absentee ballot fraud, but the news came too late to meet the deadline for asking the courts for a new election.

Absentee voting also corrupts the secret ballot. Because an absentee ballot is "potentially available for anyone to see, the perpetrator of coercion can ensure it is cast 'properly,' unlike a polling place, where a voter can promise he will vote one way but then go behind the privacy curtain and vote his conscience," notes John Fortier, a scholar at the American Enterprise Institute, in his new book, *Absentee and Early Voting*.

The need for safeguards against strong-arm tactics was proved in the 2003 mayoral race in East Chicago, Indiana. The challenger George Pabey defeated the eight-term incumbent, Robert Patrick, among Election Day voters, but lost by 278 votes after some 2,000 absentee votes were tabulated.

Investigators for Pabey turned up repeated instances of coercion and vote buying. Shelia Pierce allowed a Patrick campaign operative to fill out her absentee ballot in exchange for a $100 job at the polls. She said the operative later threatened her to keep her from testifying. Elisa Delrio said a local official offered her a similar job and even brought her absentee ballot to her hospital bed, where she was recovering from surgery. But after she wound up voting for Pabey and handed her ballot to the official, it promptly disappeared. The Indiana Supreme Court concluded that it was impossible to know who had won the election and ordered a revote a year later. Pabey won with 65 percent of the vote and was sworn in as mayor.

Abuses such as those in East Chicago can occur because many states allow political parties to collect applications for absentee ballots, and several allow them to collect the completed ballots. Most states even let campaign workers assist voters in filling out the ballots if they ask for help.

Party operatives "tend to target people who are elderly, infirm, low-income, non-English-speaking," says Jeffrey Garfield, executive director of Connecticut's Election Enforcement Commission. He notes that absentee ballot fraud has been a persistent problem in his state for years and in Hartford alone has resulted in the arrest of at least eight city politicians, including a state representative who in 2005 pleaded guilty to inducing elderly residents of a housing complex to vote for him.

Robert Pastor, director of the Center for Democracy and Election Management at American University and a 2004 John Kerry campaign adviser, says that laws allowing third-party handling of absentee ballots clearly need to be changed. "They represent an invitation for mischief, which many other countries don't allow," he told me following a hearing on election fraud and intimidation conducted by the U.S. Commission on Civil Rights.

The 2001 National Commission on Federal Election Reform, a bipartisan group co-chaired by Gerald Ford and Jimmy Carter, found that local election officials have grown sloppy in handling absentee ballots. "Most states do not routinely check signatures either on applications or on returned ballots, just as most states do not verify signatures or require proof of identity at the polls," noted John Mark Hansen, the director of research for the commission's report.

The commission concluded that absentee ballots do not satisfy five essential criteria for sound and honest elections:

- Assure the privacy of the secret ballot and protection against coerced voting.
- Verify that only duly registered voters cast ballots.
- Safeguard ballots against loss or alteration.
- Assure their prompt counting.
- Foster the communal aspect of citizens voting together.

John Fortier of AEI has some suggestions on how to retain the convenience of pre–Election Day voting but with a lower risk of fraud and intimidation. He suggests that states expand hours at polling places for early voting, but only during the ten days before Election Day. New computer software can be used to match signatures on absentee ballots with registration records and flag those that raise concerns. States could require that every voter enclose a fingerprint or photocopy of some form of identification, not necessarily a photo ID. States should hire independent investigators to interview a sample of voters about potential coercion or intimidation.

Numerous analysts, from George Will on the right to Norman Ornstein on the left, have decried the transformation of voting into an act of convenience rather than communal pride. Absentee ballots not only dispense with the privacy curtain of the voting booth, but, as Will notes, "consign to private spaces the supreme moment of public choice. Election Day should be the exhilarating central episode of our civic liturgy."

If the present trends continue, we will become a nation where half of us vote on Election Day and the other half ... well, whenever. While that may not bother some people, it won't be good for democracy if a flood of absentee ballots means the country will have to endure a slew of lawsuits and recounts that could delay the final results of the next election for weeks. Election Day could once again become Election Month before we know who won the White House this year.

Liberals' Second Thoughts

Although most complaints about absentee voting come from Republicans and election officials, a growing number of Democrats are questioning the practice. In Washington State, a computer programmer, Jason Osgood, is running as a Democrat for secretary of state by campaigning against the state's move to virtually all mail-in balloting.

Melody Rose, a liberal professor at Oregon State University, is a severe critic of that state's 100 percent mail-in ballot law. She says it hasn't raised turnout and doesn't save money because it merely shifts the cost from the state to the voter, who must pay for increasingly expensive postage to deliver the ballot. And she believes that vote-by-mail "brings a perpetual risk of systemic fraud." Ballots can easily be stolen from mailboxes, and registered voters who don't vote wouldn't bother to alert election officials if they didn't get one.

Ballot security has been promised by the new law but is not always delivered. Rose herself once stopped by a library after hours to deposit her ballot, only to find an overflowing bin of ballots in the lobby. She could have taken all of them to her car and done some creative pruning based on where people lived or their gender. And on Election Day 2000, witnesses in Pioneer Courthouse Square in Portland saw campaign workers offering people ballots from baskets and then saying they would deliver the ballots to voting centers. As a liberal, Rose also believes that mail-in voting diminishes the sense of community. "When we dig our ballot out from the junk mail and credit-card offers, only to vote while watching the latest rendition of 'Survivor,' we cheapen the process and deprive ourselves of a simple reminder of our collective responsibility," she writes. "True reform needs to increase the perceived importance and relevance of voting, not diminish it."

Boulder, Colorado, a classic university town populated largely by liberals, experimented with a mail-in ballot in November 2001 and suffered a debacle. KCNC-TV in Denver reported that thousands of ballots were mailed to incorrect addresses, to residents who had moved away and even to the dead. Clerks also rejected a thousand ballots after they were filled out and sent back by voters. In addition, more than one outraged civil libertarian couldn't understand why many of the ballots were improperly opened, allowing election workers to examine them and know how someone had voted. Linda Flack, manager of the Boulder County Elections Division, apologized for the breach of security and vowed it would not happen again.

Loose absentee laws don't increase turnout; they make fraud easier; they alter campaigns in strange ways. And as we shall see, in 2000 they hurt the Democrats more profoundly than the butterfly ballots, hanging chads and other well-remembered epiphenomena of Florida.

How Al Gore Could Have Won Florida

In 2001, a media consortium's examination of Florida's 170,000 disputed ballots again provided some evidence that George W. Bush won the state under all conventional recounting standards. While the consortium's findings are diluted by the fact that it couldn't find 1 percent of the disputed ballots, its likely conclusion is that Al Gore could have won only if highly elastic counting methods were deployed— the very sort, in fact, that Gore never asked for in court.

But there is one other scenario under which Gore could very plausibly have won: if new liberalized absentee and early voting laws had not been in place. I'm not just talking about the military ballots that Democrats got beaten up for challenging. One-quarter of all votes in the 2000 election were cast either absentee or in early voting. There is evidence that if more of those voters had cast their ballots on Election Day, Gore would have picked up additional votes.

Analysts agree that Gore had a last-minute surge in support, fueled in part by negative reaction to the news of George W. Bush's 1976 arrest for driving under the influence, which came out five days before Election Day. If more people had cast ballots on that day rather than earlier, Gore would probably have become president. The DUI incident hurt Bush. A Gallup poll indicated that 10 percent of independents were "less likely" to vote for Bush, and exit polls showed 28 percent found the issue very or somewhat important. Karl Rove, Bush's top strategist, told a symposium that the incident cost his boss the popular vote and at least one state. Luckily for him, the fact that more than half the states had either liberalized their absentee voting rules or allowed early voting meant that many voters had already "locked in" their preference before the DUI revelations. There was no way they could change their vote.

One doesn't even have to discuss Florida to ponder what might have been. Tennessee allowed people to vote at government offices starting three weeks before the election. Gore lost his home state because "he did not pay enough attention to it and was late in making personal appearances and putting up TV ads," notes Roger Simon of *U.S. News & World Report.* Because a full 36 percent of Tennessee's voters cast their ballots before Election Day, "many of them missed Gore's attempt to win the state."

Absentee voters, by definition, can't be included in surveys of voters as they exit the polls. Loose absentee laws make exit polls much less reliable, leading to voter anger if they are proven wrong. In Florida, *Brill's Content* found that "Voter News Service, and the networks it works for, failed so spectacularly because it didn't factor in the massive shifts in how

Americans vote." VNS clearly underestimated the number of absentee voters in Florida, ultimately well over 10 percent of the total. It retracted its first call of Florida for Gore at 10:13 P.M. by telling the networks: "We are still examining the absentee vote." Murray Edelman, the editorial director of VNS, admitted to his board on November 14, "The biggest problem in the model is that we did not correctly anticipate the impact of the absentee vote."

Democrats might do better to look for ways to reform the voting system that would actually improve elections, instead of just making sure the laws do not benefit Republicans. The Republicans might wish to join the critical scrutiny of early or absentee voting, for the best evidence suggests that it no longer favors the GOP.

As Democrats have found more success with upper-income voters—George W. Bush won just over half of those earning more than $100,000 a year in both 2000 and 2004—the old GOP advantage among absentee voters has faded. Indeed, it was late-counted absentee votes that increased Gore's popular-vote lead of 190,000 nationwide on election night to 539,000 in the final count. Remember that we could see 30 percent of votes cast by mail or in early voting this year, up from only 5 percent or 10 percent in 1980. John McCain might find himself leading in the popular vote on election night, only to lose it when the absentees are all counted in the days that follow.

Absentee voting used to be available only to those legitimately out of town or physically unable to vote in person. Recently, thirteen states have allowed residents to vote 17 to 21 days before Election Day. At least eighteen other states have opened absentee voting to all comers. Oregon has abolished the polling place altogether and switched to 100 percent mail-in voting. As the arguments against promiscuous absentee or early voting mount, it is time to rethink this trend.

Three

From Little Oaks
Grows a Mighty Acorn

ENNIS DIMARCO, THE REGISTRAR OF VOTERS IN JEFFERSON County, Louisiana, a New Orleans suburb, couldn't believe his eyes.

It was May 2008. A suspicious registration card from a new voter had just landed on his desk. But the card was made out in DiMarco's own name and listed his office's post office box as the address. It identified him as a male, a Democrat and an African American. Part of DiMarco was amused, because he is both white and a Republican. He also couldn't help but smile that whoever had filled out the form had "flattered me by making me younger—I did appreciate that."

But DiMarco was less amused by the fact that the phony registration lying in front of him was just part of a slew of suspect forms his office and those in other Louisiana counties had to deal with in the summer of 2008. "Registrars have begun to see a disturbing pattern of misinformation on the forms, including duplicates, cards filled out with different colors of ink, or using the names of pets and dead people," reported the *New Orleans Times-Picayune*. DiMarco complained that he had already burned through most of his postal budget because so many of the error-filled registration cards sent out had to be returned.

In Louisiana, the flood of suspect forms was the product of efforts by Voting Is Power, a national Democratic Party effort,

47

and ACORN (Association of Community Organizations for Reform Now), which promotes voting in low-income areas. Both groups claimed that massive voter registration drives were necessary to make sure no one was excluded from the political process. Silas Lee, a New Orleans political ally, dismissed the false registrations as the work of would be-comedians. "You have some people who have a distorted sense of humor," he told the *Times-Picayune*. Indeed, the message from the groups to local registrars was: *Get over it*. "Instead of throwing up complaints, they should be working to get as many people as possible registered," asserted Matthew Miller, a spokesman for the Democratic Senatorial Campaign Committee.

But the job of handling legitimate voters is needlessly complicated by phony registrations. In Shreveport, Louisiana, registrar Ernie Roberson reported that only 2,200 of the 6,000 forms his office had received were valid. "I have one lady, I have five applications on her," he moaned. Roberson expressed concern that the invalid cards might trip up legitimate voters when they try to vote. "You'll just have utter bedlam at some of these polls," he warned.

Indeed, Jacques Berry, a spokesman for Jay Dardenne, Louisiana's secretary of state, says that groups registering voters should take responsibility for their actions. He suggested their workers should "be educated enough [in proper procedures] to not leave the house until the card is in order." Others questioned the register-at-all-costs approach. "You're getting down to people that are just hard-core disengaged," warns John Maginnis, a respected local political analyst. "If you get these voters on the rolls, the question is how many of them are likely voters." Or, some would add, an open invitation for mischief.

Much of the mischief involving voter registration efforts seems to originate with ACORN, the nation's largest openly radical group, with an annual budget of over $40 million and chapters in eight hundred poor neighborhoods. It owns two "social justice" radio stations, a law office and a low-income housing corporation, and it has contracts for services with a host of trade unions. Run for the last thirty-eight years by Wade Rathke, a union organizer, ACORN is best known for its campaigns against Wal-Mart and for leading initiatives to raise the minimum wage. Its messianic mission statement boasts that it "stands virtually alone in its dedication to organizing the poor and powerless."

In reality, ACORN has a New Left–inspired agenda that Sol Stern—a former editor of the 1960s radical *Ramparts* magazine who has repudiated the New Left—calls "anti-capitalism, central planning, victimology and government handouts." In an article in the Manhattan Institute's *City Journal*, Stern traces ACORN's inspiration to the 1960s National Welfare Rights Organization, which tried to use poor, unwed mothers to foment a revolution. It would send them to engage in sit-ins and disruptions of government offices to demand an end to "oppressive" eligibility restrictions on government aid. One of the NWRO's young organizers, Wade Rathke, went on to found ACORN.

In the 1970s, ACORN discovered a pot of gold in the Community Reinvestment Act, which mandated that banks doing business in a city had to invest some of their capital in poorer neighborhoods. The CRA allowed community groups to file complaints about violations of the act that could delay or even kill bank mergers. As one nonprofit umbrella group observed, "To avoid the possibility of a denied or delayed application, lending institutions have an incentive to make formal agreements with community organizations." First in line on many occasions was ACORN, which has reaped hundreds of thousands of dollars in donations from institutions such as J.P. Morgan and Chase. In 1993, ACORN created a $55 million, eleven-city lending program for affordable housing, which it administers; the program is currently financed by fourteen major banks.

Flush with cash, ACORN is free to plow money into ostensibly nonpartisan voter outreach efforts. In 2004 alone, the organization, along with its sister organization Project Vote, claimed to have registered 1.15 million new voters and deployed 4,000 get-out-the-vote workers on Election Day.

But these voter registration efforts have been plagued by scandal, from Ohio to Washington State to New Mexico. At least two former Florida-based ACORN employees accused the group of illegal practices. Mac Stuart, who was a field operative in Miami, claimed that ACORN failed to deliver registration cards that were marked "Republican," accepted applications from felons, and falsified information. Joe Johnson, a former ACORN consultant, told the *St. Petersburg Times* two weeks before the 2004 election that he quit working with the group because of his concern that ACORN was not turning in complete voter cards.

One of the most serious cases involving ACORN came out of Seattle, where prosecutors in July 2007 indicted seven ACORN workers. They were accused of submitting phony registration forms in what Washington's secretary of state, Sam Reed, called "the worst case of voter-registration fraud" in the state's history. (Three of the seven pleaded guilty later that year.) The list of "voters" registered in Washington included former House Speaker Dennis Hastert, *New York Times* columnists Frank Rich and Tom Friedman, and actress Katie Holmes, as well as nonexistent people with nonsensical names such as Stormi Bays and Fruto Boy. The addresses used for the fake names were local homeless shelters. Given that the state doesn't require the showing of any identification before voting, it is entirely possible that people could have voted illegally using some of those names.

Local officials refused to accept the registrations because they had been delivered after the 2006 registration deadline of October 7. Initially, ACORN officials demanded that the registrations be accepted and threatened to sue King County (Seattle) officials if they were tossed out. But in early November 2006—just after four ACORN registration workers were indicted on charges of fraud in Kansas City, Missouri—the group reversed its position and said the registrations should be rejected. But by then, local election workers had a reason to scrutinize the forms carefully, and they uncovered the fraud. Of the 1,805 names submitted by ACORN, over 97 percent were found to be invalid.

The King County prosecutor, Dan Satterberg, said that in lieu of charging ACORN itself as part of the registration fraud case, he worked out an agreement by which the group paid $25,000 to reimburse the costs of the investigation and formally agree to tighten supervision of its activities, which Satterberg said were plagued by "lax oversight."

Another State, Another Scandal

In Kansas City, Missouri, where the four indicted ACORN workers pleaded guilty to committing registration fraud, only 40 percent of the 35,000 registrations submitted by the group turned out to be bogus. ACORN claims that it brought the Kansas City fraud to light; but Melody Powell, chairman of the Kansas City Board of Elections, calls this claim "seriously misleading." Her own staff first took the evidence to the FBI, she says, and only then did ACORN help identify the perpetrators. "It's a potential recipe for fraud," she says of the group's registration drive, noting that "anyone can find a voter card mailed to a false apartment building address lying around a lobby and use it to vote." Powell also worries that legitimate voters who were registered a second time by someone else under a false address might find it difficult to vote.

At another stop in the scandal tour, eight ACORN workers in St. Louis pleaded guilty to federal election fraud in April 2008 for filing false voter registration forms. St. Louis election officials were so inundated with bogus ACORN-generated voter registrations that they mailed a letter to five thousand registrants, requesting the recipients to contact them. Fewer than forty responded.

ACORN's Wade Rathke attacked the officials as "slop buckets" and claimed they had "broken the law in trying to discourage new voters illegally." City officials scoffed at that charge. They said it's up to ACORN to explain why over a thousand addresses listed on its registrations don't exist. "We met twice with ACORN before their drive, but our requests completely fell by the wayside," Matt Potter (Democrat), the city's deputy elections director, told me. His election clerks were already putting in thirteen-hour work days, he said, and "dumping this on them isn't fair." In the past, several Democrats, including Mayor Francis Slay, have complained about bloated voter rolls leading to stolen votes. ACORN insists that any problems stem from dishonest former employees and that it is implementing a new "quality control" program to avoid future problems. Rathke says he actively cooperated with a 2006 federal probe into its Kansas City operation and alerted prosecutors to registration problems in other states.

Rathke told me that Missouri's problems came about because his organizers were required to turn in all registrations within seven days of being collected "even if the name on them was Donald Duck," and that state law discouraged them from sending copies of the forms out of state to ACORN's Little Rock office, which would have done quality-control checks.

Election officials say that ACORN was responsible for policing its own work. Current and former ACORN employees say the problems that crop up around its activities are no accident. "There's no quality control on purpose, no checks and balances," says Nate Toler, who until late 2006 was head organizer of an ACORN campaign against Wal-Mart in Merced, California. In 2004 he worked on an ACORN voter drive in Missouri, and he says ACORN statements are not to be taken at face value: "The internal motto is 'We don't care if it's a lie, just so long as it stirs up the conversation.'" Toler told me he expected to be attacked as a disgruntled employee. "I may have my head chopped off for telling the truth," he said.

Indeed, in 2006 Toler filed a complaint with the Equal Employment Opportunity Commission alleging that ACORN has consistently promoted whites to management positions over equally qualified blacks. His allegations are backed by three former ACORN employees who have filed similar EEOC complaints. One of them, Sashanti Bryant of Detroit, was a community organizer for ACORN. She told me the organization has a problem paying employees on time and has almost no minorities in its upper echelons. Loretta Barton, until June 2008 a lead ACORN organizer from Dayton, Ohio, and another EEOC complainant, told me that "all ACORN wanted from registration drives was results." Barton alleges that when she and her co-workers asked about forming a union, they were slapped down: "We were told if you get a union, you won't have a job."

There is some history here: In 2003, the National Labor Relations Board ordered ACORN to rehire and pay restitution to three employees it had illegally fired for trying to organize a union.

In response, Rathke told me he is neutral on internal union-organizing efforts and that "when you're dealing with thousands of employees a year you'll have some who complain." He also said the four complaints lodged with the EEOC had all been dismissed. When told this wasn't the case, he said "there may be some loose ends to be tied up.... I'm not going to impugn any of the people involved." Still, ACORN is vulnerable to charges that it doesn't practice what it preaches. Its manual for minimum-wage campaigns says it intends "to push for as high a wage as possible." But it doesn't pay those wages. In 2004, for example, ACORN won a $9.50-an-hour minimum wage in Santa Fe, New Mexico, but paid its organizers $25,000 a year for a required fifty-four-hour week—amounting to $8.90 an hour. In 2008, ACORN had workers in Missouri sign contracts saying they would be "working up to 80 hours over seven days of work." Rathke says, "We pay as much as we can. If people can get more elsewhere, we wish them well." In 1995, ACORN unsuccessfully sued California to be exempt from the minimum wage, claiming that "the more that ACORN must pay each individual outreach worker ... the fewer outreach workers it will be able to hire." Rathke acknowledges that higher wages can cost some jobs but says the raises for other workers are worth it.

The Grapes of Rathke

This year, ACORN helped convince Congress to create an "affordable housing trust fund," which would provide a permanent pool of money, some of it to be allocated to low-income housing groups like the ones ACORN supports. The trust fund would be created by diverting 1.2 basis points of the interest income earned by the government-sponsored housing enterprises Fannie Mae and Freddie Mac. The total would be about $500 million a year. As John Berlau of the Competitive Enterprise Institute noted, "the holes in this 'trust fund' would allow the money to be easily siphoned off to liberal activist groups such as ACORN for lobbying and even political campaigning."

Given the fungibility of housing grant money, this is a real concern. Previous federal grants to ACORN have been highly controversial. In 1994, the ACORN Housing Corporation (AHC) was given a $1.1 million grant by AmeriCorps, the federal volunteer agency. In applying for the grant, the housing group claimed it was completely separate from ACORN. But the inspector general for AmeriCorps found just a year later that "AHC used AmeriCorps grant funds to benefit ACORN either directly or indirectly." She found several instances of cost shifting from ACORN's political lobbying group to the housing entity, and also found several instances of steering recipients of housing counseling into ACORN memberships. The grant was quickly terminated. A revived stream of federal cash to a group that so often fails audits would invite trouble.

Many on Capitol Hill agree. Charles Grassley, as chairman of the Senate Finance Committee, sent a letter in 2006 to the IRS asking the agency to investigate ACORN and allied groups for possibly misusing their tax status for political purposes.

On his blog, Wade Rathke dismisses criticism of ACORN as "major league political harassment . . . crazy words." Lashing out at critics, says Nate Toler, the ACORN dissident, is "just Wade being Wade, engaging in the politics of distraction." Another former ACORN employee says the group has become a "cult" under Rathke and must increasingly take bigger risks in order to grow. What risks it might take in pursuit of its agenda in 2008 can only be surmised—but the evidence so far is that ACORN may be up to its old tricks and perhaps even coming up with some new ones.

ACORN's president, John James, told reporters in 2007 that his group will cooperate fully with election officials to make sure "no one is trying to pull a fast one on us." In an official statement he said, "We are looking to the future. Voter participation is a vital part of our work to increase civic participation."

Four

Barack Obama and ACORN: Perfect Together

FOR ALL ITS CONTROVERSIAL PRACTICES AND HARD-NOSED tactics, it's striking that both Barack Obama and Hillary Clinton have so much in common with ACORN, the hard-left community organizing group at the center of so many vote fraud scandals.

But both Clinton and Obama were admirers of the man who helped inspire ACORN's tactics—Saul Alinsky, the "father" of community organizing. His approach was that the goal of revolutionaries should be to get the downtrodden to be angry enough with their condition to demand its betterment; he called it "rubbing raw the sores of discontent." In his book *Rules for Radicals*, written shortly before his death in 1973, Alinsky acknowledged his debt to Lucifer, "the very first radical," who "rebelled against the establishment and did it so effectively that he at least won his own kingdom." He called his book "a step toward a science of revolution" that was explicitly built on the tactics of Machiavelli. "The Prince was written by Machiavelli for the Haves on how to hold power. Rules for Radicals is written for the Have-nots on how to take it away."

When it came to the best way to achieve revolution, Alinsky explicitly argued for moral relativism in fighting the establishment: "In war the end justifies almost any means." Specifically, "the practical revolutionary will understand ...

[that] in action, one does not always enjoy the luxury of a decision that is consistent both with one's individual conscience and the good of mankind."

Hillary Clinton met three times with Alinsky as a college student and wound up writing her honors thesis at Wellesley on him: "There Is Only the Fight ... An Analysis of the Alinsky Model." Before Bill Clinton announced for president, she ordered that the ninety-two-page work be locked up so scholars wouldn't have access to it. But a copy leaked out a few years ago and we learned that in her conclusion, Hillary Clinton wrote: "If the ideals Alinsky espouses were actualized, the result would be social revolution. . . . Alinsky is regarded by many as the proponent of a dangerous socio/political philosophy. As such he has been feared—just as Eugene Debs or Walt Whitman or Martin Luther King has been feared, because each embraced the most radical of political faiths—democracy."

Hmmm ... comparing Saul Alinsky to Martin Luther King would cause anyone who knew him in Chicago to react with disbelief or laughter. Rev. King was an apostle of nonviolence, and while firm in his moral outrage against segregation, he did not belittle or smear his opponents. Alinsky on the other hand frequently had his followers employ megaphones to hurl insults and curses at adversaries. Among the "abrasive tactics" that Hillary Clinton noted approvingly in her thesis were his decision to send activists to picket the suburban homes of landlords and the dumping of garbage outside the city's sanitation commission.

In her senior year, in October 1968, Clinton was offered a job by Alinsky as a community organizer with his Industrial Areas Foundation. She turned it down, preferring to clerk at a radical law firm in the Bay Area instead and then attend Yale Law School, the better to change the system from within.

Hillary Clinton would later remember Alinsky fondly in meetings she attended as First Lady. She even lent her name to projects endorsed by Alinsky's IAF, and raised money and attended events for another Alinsky affiliate.

Clinton also aided ACORN, a classic Alinsky-style group, supporting its efforts to win government grants during the 1990s. In 1993 she pushed for her husband, President Bill Clinton, to make ACORN's proposed "Motor Voter" national registration law his top legislative priority. Indeed, "Motor Voter," which mandated mail-in registrations and restricted the trimming of outdated voter rolls, became the very first bill signed into law in the Clinton administration.

A little less than two decades later, a twenty-three-year-old Columbia University graduate named Barack Obama answered a want ad placed by a group called the Calumet Community Religious Conference, run by Alinsky disciples. It needed a black organizer for a dozen churches to help local residents develop tactics that would turn them into political activists. His years working as a community organizer in Chicago profoundly influenced Obama, even if he ultimately rejected Alinsky's disdain for electoral politics and, like Hillary Clinton, chose to work from within the system. "Obama embraced many of Alinsky's tactics and recently said his years as an organizer gave him the best education of his life," wrote Peter Slevin of the *Washington Post* in 2007. He noted that the two Democratic candidates' "common connection to Alinsky is one of the striking aspects of their biographies."

Their connection to ACORN is also a common thread, though Obama would be tied far more closely to the organization than Clinton.

As early as 1993, the year after Obama returned to Chicago to become a public interest lawyer after graduating from Harvard Law School, he was recruited by ACORN to run a successful voter registration drive for the ACORN affiliate Project Vote. He took time off from his law firm to run the project, which registered 135,000 new voters and was considered integral to the victory of Carol Moseley Braun as the first black senator from Illinois while at the same time it claimed to conduct only "nonpartisan" activities.

Obama became ACORN's attorney in 1995 when he sued on their behalf to force Governor Jim Edgar, a Republican, to implement the "Motor Voter" law in Illinois. That success led him to become a frequent trainer of ACORN staff. After he joined the board of the Woods Fund, a liberal foundation, Obama saw to it that substantial grants were given to ACORN.

In 1996, when Obama filled out a questionnaire listing the groups that would provide him with key support in his campaign for the Illinois Senate, he put ACORN first (and it was not an alphabetical list). Once in the U.S. Senate, Obama became the leading critic of voter ID laws, the overturning of which was the top priority of ACORN at the federal level. In 2007, in a speech to ACORN's leaders prior to their political arm's endorsement of him for president, Obama was effusive in his praise:

> I come out of a grassroots organizing background. That's what I did for three and a half years before I went to law school. That's the reason I moved to Chicago—to organize. So this is something that I know personally, the work you do, the importance of it. I've been fighting alongside of ACORN on issues you care about my entire career. Even before I was an elected official, when I ran Project Vote in Illinois, ACORN was smack dab in the middle of it, and we appreciate your work.

ACORN has responded to the challenge of the Obama presidential campaign. While Jerry Kellman of ACORN told the Capital Research Center that the group's 501(c)(3) non-profit tax status prevents it from being involved other than through its political arm, he acknowledged that "lots of grass-roots members" are backing Obama.

ACORN also runs something called "Camp Obama," which trains campaign volunteers in the same tactics that Obama honed as a community organizer. "We want you to stop thinking about Barack Obama and be Barack Obama," is how ACORN's Jocelyn Woodards sums up the two-day training program for applicants. Another program, called the Obama Organizing Fellows, is designed to train people in how to "organize in a community, working in conjunction with grassroots leaders and campaign staff." Kellman has said that the Obama campaign uses elements of both the practical and aggressive Alinsky method, and the visionary "movement" style that Obama himself now emphasizes.

For his part, Obama continues to press ACORN's legislative concerns. In the summer of 2008, he was a major supporter of a Democratic housing bill that would provide $200 million to community groups counseling homeowners who face foreclosure. Critics pointed out that much of the money would be destined for ACORN and the liberal Hispanic group La Raza. Once a community organizer, then a foundation grant-maker and now a lobbyist for direct government funding, Barack Obama has been with ACORN throughout his career. In return, ACORN is pledging to spend $35 million this year registering voters—both real and fictive. Should Obama become president, look for ACORN to have a vastly more ambitious legislative agenda, and for Obama to be responsive.

Playing Alinsky Hardball

Obama may come across as a smooth, soothing figure, but he learned from Alinsky's disciples in Chicago how to play hardball. In June 2008 he told a fundraiser in Philadelphia that he would match and exceed the Republican in any test of political combat. "If they bring a knife to the fight, we bring a gun," he said. "We don't have a choice but to win."

Chicago political observers recall that's how Obama felt in 1995, when his political career was just getting off the ground. Obama had done everything right to position himself for a seat in the Illinois Senate. He had impressive academic credentials, three years of community organizing under his belt, a membership in Rev. Jeremiah Wright's Trinity United megachurch, labor union support and even key financial backers among Chicago's politically connected business leaders who were always looking for people who would appreciate their point of view.

There was even a vacancy in the state senate district that included Obama's Hyde Park condo. The state senator, Alice Palmer, decided to run in the special election for the area's congressional seat that was held in November 1995. She met with Obama prior to announcing and in September informally endorsed him as her designated successor. Then things went awry. Senator Palmer came in a poor third in the congressional race and was immediately urged by her supporters to file for re-election to the state senate. She met with Obama again, and since he had not yet formally announced his candidacy, she asked him if he would step aside and allow her to run for another term. Obama politely but firmly turned her down, saying he was in the race to stay.

This prompted Senator Palmer to scramble to secure the 757 valid signatures she needed on her nomination petitions. On December 18, the deadline for filing, she submitted 1,580 signatures, more than twice the required number. Obama reacted quickly but behind the scenes. He dispatched two lawyers to lead a team to pore over Palmer's petitions and those of the three other candidates who had filed for the seat, to see if they could be challenged and their nomination petitions declared invalid.

The tactic was entirely legal, but it had rarely been used in an attempt to purge so many candidates off the ballot and leave just one standing. Ronald Davis, an Obama consultant whom the candidate called his "guru of petitions," recalls a brief conversation he had with his boss. "I said, 'Barack, I'm going to knock them all off.' He said, 'What do you need?'" The two men quickly agreed to hire Tom Johnson, a respected attorney who had offered Obama legal advice when he was trying to *add* names to Chicago's voter rolls as part of ACORN's Project Vote in 1993. Obama's minions were firm in questioning every signature they could, using voter lists that were more up-to-date than the ones used by the other candidates in circulating their petitions.

At least one contender, Gha-is Askia, admits that his workers may have submitted signatures that were flawed or fraudulent without his knowledge. But he told the *Chicago Tribune* that Obama's tactics still rankled him: "Why say you're for a new tomorrow, then do old-style Chicago politics to remove legitimate candidates?" he asked. "He talks about honor and democracy, but what honor is there in getting rid of every other candidate so you can run scot-free? Why not let the people decide?"

Alice Palmer goes further, claiming that enough of the signatures she filed were valid for her to stay on the ballot, but she lacked Obama's legal and financial resources to challenge the ruling that booted her off. Remembering what happened, Palmer showed up this year on the campaign trail with Hillary Clinton to support her candidacy.

Obama told the *Washington Post* that he regrets so much ill feeling resulted from his election challenges. "There's a legitimate argument to be made that you shouldn't create barriers to people getting on the ballot," he told the *Chicago Tribune*. "To my mind, we were just abiding by the rules that had been set up."

So the candidate who has called for the most open political process possible and who dismisses complaints of vote fraud even in notoriously dodgy Chicago's precincts owes his first political office to his ability to detect fraud and throw every single one of his opponents off the ballot. Barack Obama may call for change, but he started his political career practicing pure chutzpah.

Five

The Battle for Photo ID

GROUND ZERO IN THE FIGHT OVER VOTE FRAUD AND THE security measures taken by state election officials to prevent it has been the litigation filed over the photo identification laws passed by the Georgia and Indiana legislatures. Congress itself argued over the merits of requiring identification for voters when it was debating the Help America Vote Act of 2002, or HAVA. This legislation arose from the aftermath of the fight in Florida in the 2000 presidential election. It contains a series of new federal requirements intended to reform the election process, such as requiring states to implement computerized statewide voter registration lists and to provide registered voters with provisional ballots. Congress also, for the first time in history, appropriated federal funding for state and local election officials to help them implement HAVA's requirements, such as encouraging them to replace their punch-card voting machines, whose hanging chads were the subject of much controversy in the 2000 election.

The biggest fight during the HAVA debate in Congress was over voter ID—and the debate was so fierce between the Republican and Democratic senators and congressmen that it almost sank the bill. Republicans wanted all voters to show a photo ID; Democrats did not want any ID requirement at all. A compromise was finally reached in Section 303(b) of HAVA, which created the first national, although limited, voter ID requirement. It mandates that individuals who register by mail and who have not previously voted in a federal election must present a current and valid photo identification or a copy of a current utility bill, bank statement, paycheck, government check or other government document showing the name and address of the voter. If the person votes by mail, he has to provide a copy of such identification with his absentee ballot. Even this ID requirement, however, will not apply to anyone who provides either a driver's license number or the last four digits of a Social Security number on the registration form if the state is able to match that information with an existing state identification record bearing the same number, name and date of birth as provided in the registration form.

The weaknesses in this federal requirement are obvious. It applies only to voters who register by mail and only the first time they vote in a federal election. But under Motor Voter registration, no one—not even those who register in person with county election officials—is required to present any type of ID. Furthermore, many states have concluded that the ID requirement of HAVA does not apply if a group conducting a registration drive turns in registration forms directly to election officials instead of mailing them in, despite the fact that no election official has ever seen the individual who is registering and no check has been made of the voter's authenticity. Moreover, there have been numerous instances of organizations such as ACORN submitting fraudulent forms when they conduct registration drives. Since HAVA's requirement applies only the first time a mail-in registrant goes to vote in a federal election, there is nothing to prevent an imposter from voting in his place in subsequent elections. Finally, the other acceptable documents, such as utility bills and bank statements, can be produced easily by anyone with a computer and a color printer.

When Georgia and Indiana were implementing some of the new state legislation required by HAVA, they decided to require voters to show a government-issued photo ID. Congress had specified that all of the HAVA requirements were "minimum requirements" and nothing prevented a state from establishing stricter requirements, including an ID provision.

Georgia

Georgia had actually implemented its first voter ID law for in-person voting in 1997 when Democrats controlled the state's legislature. It listed seventeen different documents that could be used, such as a birth certificate, Social Security card, current utility bill, government check, payroll check or bank statement, and it had an exemption that allowed a voter to complete an affidavit swearing to his identity instead of producing a document. A lawyer who worked as a lobbyist in Georgia and who was there when the law was passed told me that not only did black legislators insist on the affidavit exemption, but everyone knew that the Clinton-controlled Justice Department would never approve an ID requirement without one.

Georgia had a history of disputed elections and fraudulent voting, including the infamous vote fraud that helped elect Herman Talmadge governor in 1947 when voters in places like Telfair County voted in alphabetical order or from their cemetery plots. Jimmy Carter was almost cheated out of his first election because of vote fraud by local political bosses. The dangers and threats to the security of elections were demonstrated by an analysis conducted by the *Atlanta Journal-Constitution* and WSB-TV, published in 2000, which found that more than 5,412 votes had been cast in the names of deceased voters in Georgia, sometimes on multiple occasions, over the prior twenty years, and at least 15,000 dead voters were still registered to vote. The Democratic secretary of state, Cathy Cox, tried to dismiss this finding in later years because it turned out that one of those listings was an error; the son of the deceased registered voter had been mistakenly checked in by poll officers under his father's name when he voted in Fulton County. But according to a former Fulton County election official, the secretary of state never investigated any of the other 5,411 deceased individuals on the list and never even obtained the list from the newspaper.

In 2004, Republicans won a majority in the Georgia legislature for the first time since Reconstruction. In 2005, the legislature revised the voter ID law by reducing the number of acceptable IDs to six government-issued photo IDs and eliminating the affidavit exception. Acceptable forms of ID included a driver's license issued by the Georgia Department of Driver Services (DDS) or photo ID issued by any state or by the federal government (which would include passports and college IDs issued by Georgia's university system); an employee ID issued by Georgia state government, a local government, or the federal government; a military ID; or a tribal ID. Anyone declaring indigence in an affidavit would get a photo ID from DDS free of charge, and the state was going to provide a mobile bus system to provide ID cards to locations remote from DDS offices. Voters without a photo ID at the polling place could vote using a provisional ballot; that ballot would not be counted unless the voter returned to the registrar's office with photo ID within forty-eight hours of the election.

Georgia is one of a handful of states that is required under Section 5 of the Voting Rights Act of 1965 to "preclear" any changes in its voting laws with the Civil Rights Division of the U.S. Department of Justice before the law can become effective. For the new law to pass muster, the state must show that it is not retrogressive for minorities—that it does not put them in a worse position than under the status quo. Other constitutional concerns are outside the department's jurisdiction, and the Voting Rights Act gives judicial remedies to parties who believe a law to be discriminatory. After Georgia submitted the new voter ID law, Justice precleared the law without objection in 2005 after it found that there would be no discriminatory effect on minority voters. The department relied on statistics such as the fact that there were 6.4 million holders of photo ID issued by DDS, while there were only 4.5 million registered voters in the state; racial data on the photo IDs showed that 28 percent were issued to black Georgians, slightly higher than the black percentage of the voting-age population; and student IDs issued by Georgia's university system showed that 26.8 percent of all college students were black, slightly higher than the percentage of black students in Georgia's voting-age population.

Despite these statistics, however, the decision not to object to the Georgia law was strongly criticized by a host of traditional civil rights organizations such as the National Association for the Advancement of Colored People (NAACP) and the Leadership Conference on Civil Rights, who claimed (without evidence) that the voter ID law would depress the turnout of minority voters. The preclearance of Georgia's voter ID law also became tied up in the controversy over the Justice Department's firing of U.S. attorneys in 2007, which supposedly provided further evidence that the department had been "politicized," that it was making decisions for political rather than legitimate legal reasons. In fact, Senator Barack Obama was so incensed that he placed a hold on President Bush's nominee to the Federal Election Commission, Hans von Spakovsky, who was the counsel overlooking voting matters in the Civil Rights Division when the Georgia law was approved, and wrote an editorial condemning him in a local Chicago paper.

After preclearance, a host of liberal organizations filed suit against the Georgia voter ID law, claiming it disenfranchised minority, poor and elderly voters who did not have a photo ID and could not obtain one. The organizations included Common Cause of Georgia, the League of Women Voters of Georgia, the NAACP, the Concerned Black Clergy of Metropolitan Atlanta, and two individual plaintiffs. The lawsuit claimed that the photo ID requirement unnecessarily burdened the right to vote, violating the equal protection clause of the Fourteenth Amendment, the Civil Rights Act of 1964, and Section 2 of the Voting Rights Act, and that it constituted a poll tax prohibited by the Twenty-fourth Amendment. Normally, a lawsuit filed against a law passed by a state legislature would be filed in the capital city where the legislature is located. But in a clear attempt at forum shopping to find a favorable judge—rather than risking the random assignment process for the numerous judges in the U.S. District Court for the Northern District of Georgia in Atlanta, some of whom are conservatives appointed by Republican presidents—the lawyers filed their case in Rome, Georgia. The federal court in Rome has only one federal judge. At the time, it was Harold L. Murphy, a former Democratic state legislator appointed by President Jimmy Carter and a cousin of Tom Murphy, former longtime Democratic speaker of the Georgia House of Representatives. Judge Murphy is considered to be one of the most liberal, if not the most liberal, federal judge in Georgia.

At first the plaintiffs seemed to be successful. Judge Murphy issued a preliminary injunction against the Georgia law on October 18, 2005, finding a substantial likelihood that the plaintiffs would be able to prove that the law violated the equal protection clause of the Fourteenth Amendment for poor and elderly voters or that it was a prohibited poll tax under the Twenty-fourth Amendment. Judge Murphy did not base his preliminary injunction on the Voting Rights Act claim made by the plaintiffs, however, because there was no evidence of racial discrimination in the law, a finding that upheld the Justice Department's preclearance of the law.

During its 2006 session, the Georgia legislature amended the voter ID law to make all photo IDs issued by DDS free for the asking, eliminate the indigent affidavit requirement, and allow IDs to be issued not just by DDS, but by any county registrar. The plaintiffs continued their litigation against the amended law, arguing that it still violated the same laws and constitutional amendments and that it disenfranchised voters.

Despite the claims of the plaintiffs' lawyers that there were hundreds of thousands of Georgia voters who did not have a photo ID and could not obtain one, over the course of the next two years of litigation they were unable to produce a single voter who was disenfranchised by the Georgia law. After the original litigation was filed in federal court with two named individual plaintiffs in addition to the organizational plaintiffs, one of those individuals withdrew when he found out that he would have to appear at a deposition. The remaining individual, Clara Williams, actually had a government-issued photo ID in the form of a MARTA transit card. The plaintiffs were forced to find another plaintiff when the Georgia Supreme Court ruled in a second case, filed in state court by former governor Roy Barnes (and ultimately dismissed), that a MARTA card was a valid ID for purposes of voting under the law.

This set off a scramble by the plaintiffs' lawyers, part of which was detailed in an e-mail sent out by Danny Levitas of the ACLU to his "Key Georgia Contacts" whose subject was "URGENT REQUEST FOR HELP IN THE PHOTO ID CASE." Levitas was forwarding an e-mail from Emmet Bondurant, the main lawyer representing the plaintiffs and the former head of Common Cause in Georgia. Bondurant sounded desperate to find individual voters who could be plaintiffs in his lawsuit:

[W]e need to find one or more new people who are (1) registered to vote, who normally vote in-person at a local poll in their home precincts (as opposed to voting may mail), (3) [*sic*] who do not have a Georgia driver's license, a government-issued photo ID card, or a Marta card with a photo, and (4) for whom it would be a hardship to to [*sic*] have to travel to the county registrar's office to get Georgia voter ID in order to be allowed to vote....

According to the most recent data available there are over 285,000 registered voters in Georgia who do not have a Georgia driver's license. Surely you, or someone in your organization or church knows a number of such people who do not have a car either because of their age, or simply because they are poor or disabled.

WE URGENTLY NEED YOUR HELP IN IDENTIFYING INDIVIDUALS WHO MEET THE DESCRIPTION THAT I SET FORTH ABOVE WHO WOULD BE WILLING TO BECOME PLAINTIFFS.

Despite this broad appeal, and the resources of all the different liberal organizations and churches involved in or supporting the litigation, they were able to find only two individuals to be new plaintiffs, Bertha Young and Eugene Taylor, both of whom had connections to the attorneys. The attorneys also found two other individuals to be witnesses (although not plaintiffs) who supposedly did not have photo IDs and had previously filed declarations in the federal case. Unfortunately for the lawyers, but fortunately for the voters of Georgia and the security and integrity of the election process in general, the depositions of these four individuals did not exactly go as the attorneys for Common Cause, the ACLU and the NAACP had probably hoped. In fact, the results were almost comical.

Ms. Young, for example, who was seventy-eight years old and lived only one block away from her polling place, testified that she did not have a driver's license or any other form of photo ID. However, she was employed as a housekeeper by one of the lawyers in the case, who had her picked up and driven to his house at least two days a week to do her cleaning job. Moreover, even though the lawyers were trying to claim that she could not get to a DDS office or the county registrar's office to obtain a photo ID, Ms. Young testified that she regularly went across town to her bank, passing by the registrar's office two miles from her home. In addition, her son would take her anywhere she wanted to go, and she said she would have no trouble at all obtaining a photo ID. She admitted that when her husband passed away more than thirty years ago, she was required to get a photo ID from the Rome Police Department in order to collect benefits under Social Security. Even though the photo ID had expired, she was still using it to cash checks.

The second new plaintiff, Eugene Taylor, was eighty-six years old. Taylor had been recruited as a plaintiff by his grandson, who went to law school with one of the lawyers. Taylor testified that he did not have a photo ID and did not drive, so it would be extremely difficult for him to get an ID or vote in person. However, it turned out that his lawyer had driven Taylor four hours from Screven County to Rome so he could testify in the case, passing a number of DDS locations where he could have obtained a photo ID along the way. Taylor was also forced to admit that he lived the same distance from his polling place as he did from the registrar's office where he could obtain an ID. It turned out that his daughter regularly brought him groceries and his medicine; and someone also picked him up to transport him to the farm were he worked a few times a month. To the obvious consternation of his lawyers, he admitted in the deposition that he could easily get a photo ID since his daughter could take him to the registrar's office to obtain one.

A third witness who was deposed but was not a plaintiff, Annie Johnson, was seventy-seven years old and lived in Jimmy Carter's hometown of Plains, Georgia. She had provided a declaration saying that she would not be able to get a photo ID because of health problems and difficulty traveling long distances (the nearest DDS and voter registrar offices were in Americus, about eleven miles from her residence). She had also sworn that she did not have a driver's license, Social Security card, or birth certificate.

Unfortunately for her lawyers, however, Ms. Johnson testified in her deposition that she went to Americus regularly on business and that her son or daughter or friends drove her wherever she needed to go. When she was told that the photo ID was free and that she could obtain it from her registrar's office, she said she would plan to pick one up the next time she was in Americus. She testified that she didn't think it would be difficult at all to get one, and she was prepared to do so.

When asked about her earlier declaration, Ms. Johnson could not remember signing it. Then she recalled that President Carter's deacon had come to her house with the declaration and told her she needed to sign it in order to keep voting. Throughout the deposition, she kept asking if she would go to jail because she had done something wrong by signing a declaration that was untrue—an interesting comment on the lengths to which the lawyers for the plaintiffs and President Carter's deacon would go, scaring an elderly voter into thinking she was going to lose her right to vote if she didn't help them in their case.

The final affidavit relied on by the plaintiffs was from Larry Dewberry, fifty-four years old, who lived in Fort Valley, Georgia, and had an expired driver's license, military ID and college ID. He admitted that his family drove him when he needed to go anywhere. Although the nearest DDS office was ten or twelve miles away in the town of Perry, it turned out that Dewberry lived a quarter of a mile from the voter registrar's office, and he could walk there in seven or eight minutes. When Dewberry found out during his deposition that he could obtain a photo ID at his registrar's office for free, he said that if he had known so earlier, he would already have gotten a photo ID.

The plaintiffs tried to bring into evidence the report of a supposed "expert" to support their claims that there were hundreds of thousands of Georgia voters without any photo ID. That testimony, however, was so unreliable that Judge Murphy excluded it (as happened in the Indiana case) and called it "irrelevant to the issues" in the case. The plaintiffs' expert based his claims on a comparison of the registered voter list with the driver's license list; but as Judge Murphy pointed out, the expert failed to take into account the effect of the state making free IDs available, did not consider acceptable photo IDs issued by other agencies, did not include the ability to vote absentee in his analysis, and did not take into account ineligible voters still on the registration list such as voters who had moved or died. Of course, the plaintiffs' expert did conclude that "when registered voters were examined separately by race and ethnicity, the Photo ID requirement was predicted" to have no negative effect on black or Hispanic turnout. Similarly, Judge Murphy dismissed as "far from reliable" the large numbers of registered voters who supposedly did not have an ID as reported by the former secretary of state, Cathy Cox, who had made it very clear that she opposed the voter ID law, and noted that he even mistakenly appeared on the list.

When Judge Murphy issued his final order in this case, he did so on two different grounds. First, he ruled that none of the organizations or individuals had standing to sue because none of them could show that their members or the individual plaintiffs either did not have a photo ID or could not easily obtain one. Second, he dismissed all of the constitutional and

Voting Rights Act claims. He was unpersuaded by the argument that requiring a photo ID, in and of itself, significantly burdens the right to vote:

> [A]lthough Plaintiffs claim to know of people who claim that they lack Photo ID, Plaintiffs have failed to identify those individuals. The failure to identify those individuals "is particularly acute" in light of Plaintiffs' contention that a large number of Georgia voters lack acceptable Photo ID.... As the Rokita court noted [in the Indiana photo ID case], voters who lack Photo ID undoubtedly exist somewhere, but the fact that Plaintiffs, in spite of their efforts, have failed to uncover anyone "who can attest to the fact that he/she will be prevented from voting" provides significant support for a conclusion that the Photo ID requirement does not unduly burden the right to vote.

In fact, Judge Murphy cited approvingly to the decision in the Indiana photo ID case that upheld that law, apparently because of the similarity of the claims made by the plaintiffs in Indiana to the claims made in the Georgia case:

> Plaintiffs simply have not presented sufficient admissible evidence to show that the Photo ID requirement severely burdens the right to vote. Indeed, as the court noted in Rokita: "Despite apocalyptic assertions of wholesale voter disenfranchisement, Plaintiffs have produced not a single piece of evidence of any identifiable registered voter who would be prevented from voting pursuant to [the 2006 Photo ID Act] because of his or her inability to obtain the necessary photo identification Similarly, Plaintiffs have failed to produce any evidence of any individual ... who would undergo any appreciable hardship to obtain photo identification in order to be qualified to vote."

Although he did not say so directly, Judge Murphy seemingly felt some regret over having initially issued a preliminary injunction in this case. He acknowledged that in his prior orders, he had "concluded that the Photo ID requirement severely burdened voters." But he pointed out that preliminary injunction motions take place at the early stages of litigation, when there are "more relaxed evidentiary standards. Here, however, Plaintiffs must actually prove their contentions by a preponderance of the evidence, using evidence reduced to an admissible form. Plaintiffs have failed to do so here." It seems obvious that the judge felt that he had bought into the plaintiffs' early contentions, and that they entirely failed to prove those contentions to be true by the end of the case. Similarly, Judge Murphy found in his final order that the photo ID law was rationally related to the state's interest in preventing vote fraud and he chided himself, admitting that in his previous order he had "speculated that the Photo ID requirement probably was not even rationally related to the asserted justification of preventing voting fraud. That speculation, however, is not binding on the Court and, frankly, proved to be inaccurate."

Judge Murphy had also backtracked in an earlier order on the idea of the costs associated with obtaining a photo ID card being a poll tax. Even after the Georgia legislature had made the ID card free for the asking, the plaintiffs claimed that the costs of "traveling to a registrar's office" as well as the costs for obtaining documents like a birth certificate were a "constructive" poll tax. Judge Murphy dismissed that claim, however, approvingly citing the holding of the federal district court in the Indiana photo ID case:

> This argument represents a dramatic overstatement of what fairly constitutes a "poll tax." It is axiomatic that "(e)lection laws will invariably impose some burden upon individual voters." Thus the imposition of tangential burdens does not transform a regulation into a poll tax. Moreover, the cost of time and transportation cannot plausibly qualify as a prohibited poll tax

because those same "costs" also result from voter registration and in-person voting requirements, which one would not reasonably construe as a poll tax. Plaintiffs provide no principled argument in support of this poll tax theory.

Despite the fact that Judge Murphy had dismissed all the claims as not credible, these unsubstantiated claims continue to be asserted by the lawyers who were involved in the case, creating their own urban myth. At a debate on Georgia's voter ID law at the Georgia State University College of Law in April 2008 sponsored by the Federalist Society and the American Constitution Society, eight months after the federal case was decided, Emmet Bondurant was still claiming that there were hundreds of thousands of Georgia voters who were disenfranchised by the voter ID law. The dismissal of his claim and the actual results in Georgia elections when the law became effective after the federal case was thrown out seemed to have made no impression on him at all.

For example, Karen Handel, Georgia's secretary of state, pointed out in a column in the *Atlanta Journal-Constitution* on January 18, 2008, that in two elections held in local contests after the law became effective, there had been no problems at all and there had "not been one single demonstrated deprivation of any right to vote or any other violation of a constitutional right resulting from the requirement." Similarly, Georgia had record turnout in its presidential primary on February 5, 2008, when the new photo ID law was in effect for the first time in a statewide election in Georgia. Over 2 million Georgians cast votes, nearly a million more than in the 2004 primary—the exact opposite result from that predicted by opponents of voter ID, who have claimed that requiring photo ID will depress the turnout of minority, poor and elderly voters. Not only did the turnout in Georgia go up dramatically after the photo ID law became effective, but 100,000 more votes were cast in the Democratic primary than in the Republican primary even though the overwhelming majority of black voters, who were supposedly hurt by the photo ID requirement, vote Democratic. Out of 2 million people who showed up at the polls, only 0.01 percent did not have a photo ID. Georgia even had a substantial increase in the registration of minority voters in the six months prior to the election; the registration of black males increased by more than 14 percent and of black females by more than 20 percent.

Indiana

Indiana had recurring problems with vastly inflated voter registration rolls and vote fraud in places like East Chicago, where the Indiana Supreme Court invalidated the 2003 mayoral primary because of rampant fraud, including the use of vacant lots as addresses and the casting of ballots by nonresidents. In fact, the court found that the widespread fraud had rendered the election results "inherently deceptive and unreliable." Indiana's voter rolls were among the most inflated in the nation, including over 35,000 deceased voters and 233,519 duplicate registrations, with the result that 41.4 percent of the list was considered invalid and many Indiana counties had voter registration totals that exceeded the voting-age population.

The Indiana legislature responded in 2005 by passing a photo ID law. Like Georgia's law, acceptable forms of photo ID are those issued by Indiana or the United States, which would include an unexpired driver's license, a student ID from an Indiana state college or university, a passport or a military ID. Indiana will also supply a free ID to anyone who does not have an Indiana driver's license, while voters who are over sixty-five, disabled, or confined by illness or injury may cast an absentee ballot by mail without an ID.

The Indiana Democratic Party immediately filed suit against the photo ID law, along with several organizations such as the NAACP, the Concerned Clergy of Indianapolis, and United Senior Action of Indiana. The suit claimed that the law imposed an undue burden on the right to vote, impermissibly discriminated between different classes of voters, disproportionately affected disadvantaged voters, was unconstitutionally vague, imposed a new and material requirement for voting, and was not justified by existing circumstances or evidence, all in violation of the First and Fourteenth Amendments to the Constitution.

Just as in the federal lawsuit filed against the Georgia law, however, the Indiana lawyers were unable to find any individuals who could not meet the requirements of the photo ID law—despite their claims that hundreds of thousands of Indiana voters did not have ID and would not be able to vote under the law. As the federal court said when it dismissed the case, the plaintiffs failed to find "evidence of a single, individual Indiana resident who will be unable to vote as a result of [the voter ID law] or who will have his or her right to vote unduly burdened."

The claims of some of the individual plaintiffs in the Indiana case were just as comical as in the Georgia case, to the point where one really has to wonder what the attorneys were thinking in putting them forward as plaintiffs. For example, one of the plaintiffs was an employee of the Bureau of Motor Vehicles who also worked as a judge in the polls on Election Day on behalf of the Democratic Party. Although she had originally claimed she had no photo ID, this employee of the state agency that issues driver's licenses and nondriver's photo IDs had to admit at her deposition that she did in fact have a valid driver's license. When asked about the discrepancy, she said, "I may have made a mistake there."

Another individual plaintiff had a nondriver's photo ID issued by the BMV, making it hard to understand why the attorneys would present him to the court as a plaintiff. Other individuals who claimed not to have any photo ID were almost all poll workers for the Democratic Party; there was apparently no explanation of how they could obtain employment without presenting identification as required by all other Americans. Typical were also the claims of William Crawford, a state representative who admitted that he had a photo ID, but said he had been told by a number of persons that they did not have the ID required to vote. However, he was "unable to identif[y] any such person by name to the Court." All the organizational plaintiffs like the NAACP had the same problem; their representatives kept claiming in their depositions that they had members or knew individuals who did not have photo ID, but they could never actually identify a single person without an ID.

The district court chided the plaintiffs because they "repeatedly advanced novel, sweeping political arguments which, if adopted, would require the invalidation, not only of [the voter ID law], but of other significant portions of Indiana's election code which have previously passed constitutional muster and/or to which Plaintiffs do not actually object; indeed, they offer them as preferable alternatives to the new Voter ID Law." Basically, the court accused the plaintiffs of taking a political dispute in the Indiana legislature and moving it into a judicial forum, failing "to adapt their arguments to the legal arena."

The court also criticized the plaintiffs by citing federal judge Alex Kozinski's admonition in another case against trying to use the power of "federal judges to constitutionalize our personal preferences." This was typified by individual plaintiffs like Joseph Simpson, a township trustee, who admitted he had a photo ID but was apparently a plaintiff in the lawsuit in part because "[o]n a personal basis, Simpson strongly objects to having to show his identification in order to vote." The court expressed its annoyance at "the haphazard, 'shot gun' approach utilized by the attorneys in raising these difficult issues and then leaving them unsupported by evidence or controlling legal precedent."

Once again, in a strange parallel to the Georgia lawsuit, the plaintiffs tried to enter into evidence the report of an "expert" to show that based on a comparison of the voter registration list with Indiana driver's license records, there were supposedly almost a million Indiana registered voters who did not have a photo ID. The court excluded the testimony, regarding "the analysis and conclusions set out in it as utterly incredible and unreliable." The court said it lacked the time and space to discuss in detail the numerous flaws in the supposed expert's report. In summary, however, its most significant flaws included:

> (1) failing to account for voter roll inflation, (2) comparing demographic data from different years without qualification or analysis, (3) drawing obviously inaccurate and illogical conclusions, and (4) failing to qualify the statistical estimates based on socioeconomic data.

To the extent that any of the data on which the report rested was admissible at all, it actually strengthened the state's case:

> In other words, an estimated 99% of Indiana's voting age population already possesses the necessary photo identification to vote under the requirements of [the photo ID law]. Moreover, Brace's report suggests that the fewer than 1% of individuals without acceptable Indiana photo identification are substantially concentrated in Marion County [Indianapolis], which has a metro bus system and multiple BMV branch locations thereby greatly facilitating the ability of these affected individuals to obtain the necessary photo identification.

The district court's decision was affirmed by the Seventh Circuit Court of Appeals. In commenting on the claim that there was no evidence of impersonation fraud at the polls justifying a photo ID law, the court pointed out an obvious fact:

> [T]he absence of prosecutions is explained by the endemic under enforcement of minor criminal laws (minor as they appear to the public and prosecutors, at all events) and by the extreme difficulty of apprehending a voter impersonator. He enters the polling place, gives a name that is not his own, votes, and leaves. If later it is discovered that the name he gave is that of a dead person, no one at the polling place will remember the face of the person who gave that name, and if someone did remember it, what would he do with the information? The impersonator and the person impersonated (if living) might show up at the polls at the same time and a confrontation might ensue that might lead to a citizen arrest or a call to the police who would arrive before the impersonator had fled, and arrest him. A more likely sequence would be for the impersonated person to have voted already when the impersonator arrived and tried to vote in his name. But in either case an arrest would be most unlikely (and likewise if the impersonation were discovered or suspected by comparing signatures, when that is done), as the resulting commotion would disrupt the voting. And anyway the impersonated voter is likely to be dead or in another district or precinct or to be acting in cahoots with the impersonator, rather than to be a neighbor (precincts are small, sometimes a single apartment house).

The Indiana case was appealed to the U.S. Supreme Court, which heard oral arguments on January 9, 2007. The petitioners' arguments seemed to be met with some skepticism by many of the justices. Chief Justice Roberts cited the fact that, despite the petitioners' claims of huge numbers of Indiana voters without a photo ID, "the record shows that fewer than

1 percent of people in Indiana don't have a photo ID." When their lawyer told the justices that impersonation fraud could be easily detected even without an ID because the real voters would object if someone had voted in their place, Justice Scalia bitingly observed that "[t]he people who are dead or have moved away would certainly not be objecting." Even the liberal Justice Breyer seemed skeptical of the arguments being made by the lawyer for the petitioners on how easy such fraud would be to detect:

> Someone walks in, saying: I'm Joe Smith. He doesn't say: I'm Joe Smith dead. He says, I'm Joe Smith, and he signs something. And the poll worker looks at it and the signature looks very weird. Well, what's the poll worker supposed to do? He's not going to go disrupt the election. And is there going to be a policeman there to follow this person home? Of course not.

Justice Breyer was, of course, correct about the inability of poll workers to detect impersonation fraud, except for the very rare occasions when there may be someone in the polling place who actually knows the registered voter. A newspaper in Hoboken, New Jersey, reported on just such an incident in a local election in 2007. John Branciforte, the former Zoning Board president, was on his way to a polling place when he noticed something unusual on a street corner: "two Caucasian men were standing in a semi-circle of about seven men, and were holding an envelope and handing out 3x5 index cards." One of the men receiving an index card reminded Branciforte of someone he knew. Later that morning, the same man came into the polling place and Branciforte challenged him after he signed in as a registered voter. At the challenge, the man ran out of the polling place and was later arrested by police. He admitted that he had tried to vote in the name of another voter. He lived in a homeless shelter and had been paid $10 by the "two Caucasian men" to vote in the name of a specific voter, hence the index cards.

The lawyer for the Indiana petitioners claimed that there was no evidence of any impersonation fraud "in living memory in this country." But as the former FEC commissioner Hans von Spakovsky pointed out in a study for the Heritage Foundation in March 2008, a grand jury in New York released a report in 1984 detailing a widespread vote fraud conspiracy involving impersonation fraud at the polls that operated successfully for fourteen years in Brooklyn without detection. Von Spakovsky also remarked that a voter ID requirement, besides preventing impersonation fraud at the polls, also prevents bogus votes cast on the basis of fictitious voter registrations, and votes cast by illegal aliens who are registered to vote, and double voting by individuals who are registered in more than one state.

This latter problem of double registration proved particularly embarrassing to the petitioners in the Indiana case. One of the Indiana voters who had difficulty voting because of the voter ID law and who was highlighted by the League of Women Voters in its amicus brief as a poster child for the "unbearable" burden of the law was Faye Buis-Ewing, seventy-two years old, who claimed to be a fifty-year resident of Indiana.

On the day of the oral arguments, however, an Indiana newspaper published an article detailing an interview with Ms. Buis-Ewing. It turned out that she was initially unable to vote in Indiana because when she arrived at her polling place, she tried to use a Florida driver's license as her identification. Not only did she have a Florida driver's license, but she was also registered to vote in Florida, where she and her husband owned a home. In fact, she had claimed residency in both states and received a homestead exemption on her property taxes in both states, an obvious admission of tax fraud. The point, however, is that she had claimed she was a resident of Florida and had registered to vote there, yet she was also registered to vote in Indiana and eventually did cast a vote in Indiana.

The claims by opponents of Indiana's voter ID law that it would depress the turnout of voters, particularly minority voters and the poor and elderly, suffered a blow when a University of Missouri professor published his analysis of what actually happened in Indiana elections after the ID law went into effect. Professor Jeffrey Milyo's review of turnout across the state showed that "[o]verall, voter turnout in Indiana increased about two percentage points from 2002 to 2006; however, in counties with greater percentages of minority or poor voters, turnout increased by even more, although this increase is not statistically significant." Voter ID had no negative effect on the turnout of voters, and the "only consistent and frequently significant effect of voter ID" that Milyo could find was "a positive effect on turnout in counties with a greater percentage of Democrat-leaning voters."

Milyo's findings are consistent with those of other researchers who likewise have found that voter ID laws do not affect voter turnout—contrary to the constant, unproven claims of critics. The Heritage Foundation, for example, released a data analysis of turnout in the 2004 election that showed that voter ID laws "do not have [a] negative impact on voter turnout." In general, individuals in states that require photo or other ID are just as likely to report voting as individuals in states that only require voters to state their name at their polling place. African American and Hispanic individuals in photo ID states are just as likely to report voting as are African American and Hispanic voters in non-ID states. The Heritage study was actually a reanalysis of 2004 data used by

Rutgers University's Eagleton Institute of Politics and the Moritz College of Law at Ohio State University in a voter ID study conducted under the auspices of a research grant from the U.S. Election Assistance Commission. The Eagleton Institute had concluded (it turned out wrongly) that voter ID laws do depress turnout. As Heritage pointed out, however, the Eagleton researchers (just like the "experts" in the Georgia and Indiana cases) had made basic methodological mistakes in their analysis, misclassified the voter ID laws in certain states, and even used some variables inappropriately.

A similar study by professors at the University of Delaware and the University of Nebraska at Lincoln, which examined national turnout in the 2000, 2002, 2004 and 2006 elections, at both the aggregate and the individual level, concluded that voter ID laws do not affect turnout at either level. Citing Shakespeare, the professors said that the "concerns about voter identification laws affecting turnout are much ado about nothing."

But all these academic studies would prove meaningless if the Supreme Court ruled against the concept of voter ID laws. Both supporters and opponents spent an anxious four months waiting for the high court to make up its mind.

Six

A Supreme Court Victory

I N THE ANNALS OF BALLOT INTEGRITY, APRIL 28, 2008 WILL go down as a red-letter day. It was then that the Supreme Court upheld the constitutionality of Indiana's photo ID law in a 6 to 3 decision, with the lead opinion written by Justice John Paul Stevens. The fact that one of the Supreme Court's leading liberal justices voted in favor of voter ID was probably one of the most dismaying aspects of the decision for the many liberal groups like the NAACP and the League of Women Voters who have fought against these laws.

In ruling on the constitutionality of Indiana's voter ID law—the toughest in the nation—the Supreme Court had to deal with the claim that such laws demanded the strictest of scrutiny by courts because they could disenfranchise voters. All nine justices rejected this argument in the case of *Crawford v. Marion County Election Board.* Even Justice Stephen Breyer, one of the three dissenters who would have overturned the Indiana law, wrote approvingly of the less severe ID laws of Georgia and Florida. The result is that state voter ID laws are now highly likely to pass constitutional muster.

The six justices approving the Indiana law issued two opinions, one written by Justice Stevens and joined by Chief Justice Roberts and Justice Kennedy, and a second opinion written by Justice Scalia and joined by Justices Thomas and Alito. Justice Stevens does not apply a strict scrutiny analysis as was urged by the petitioners, but a less restrictive balancing test that allows a state to present "relevant and legitimate state interests" that justify the burden that the ID law places on voters. The Court found that Indiana's interest in deterring and detecting vote fraud is unquestionably relevant to protecting the integrity and reliability of the electoral process. The state's interest in upholding public confidence in elections also has independent significance because such confidence encourages participation in the democratic process.

Stevens acknowledged that the record showed no evidence of impersonation fraud in Indiana. But he noted that "flagrant examples of such fraud in other parts of the country have been documented throughout this Nation's history by respected historians and journalists, that occasional examples have surfaced in recent years, and that Indiana's own experience with fraudulent voting in the 2003 Democratic primary for East Chicago Mayor—though perpetrated using absentee ballots and not in-person fraud—demonstrates that not only is the risk of voter fraud real but that it could affect the outcome of a close election."

The burden imposed on voters is the requirement to obtain a photo ID. Since the Indiana law provided that such IDs would be free, the inconvenience of gathering relevant documents, going to the BMV and posing for a photograph do "not qualify as a substantial burden on the right to vote, or even represent a significant increase over the usual burdens of voting." Regarding the claim that this law was passed only by Republicans to disadvantage Democrats politically, Stevens wrote that "valid neutral justifications" for a nondiscriminatory law will not be disregarded just "because partisan interests may have provided one motivation for the votes of individual legislators."

Justice Stevens chastised the dissenters for their reliance on speculation about the harmful effects of voter ID laws in general—on the specious claims that large numbers of voters, particularly minorities, do not have photo ID and that laws requiring it will cause the massive disenfranchisement of voters. In a footnote, Justice Stevens said that "[s]upposition based on extensive Internet research is not an adequate substitute for admissible evidence subject to cross-examination in constitutional adjudication."

Justice Scalia made an even stronger argument that the particular burdens that the photo ID requirement imposes on some voters are irrelevant—a warning that he would not consider any "as applied" challenges. He wrote that the law should be upheld because its overall burden is "minimal and justified." The universally applicable photo ID requirements "are eminently reasonable" and the "burden of acquiring, possessing, and showing a free photo identification is simply not severe, because it does not even represent a significant increase over the usual burdens of voting."

Justice Souter, joined by Justice Ginsburg, found the law unconstitutional because it imposes "nontrivial burdens on the voting right of tens of thousands of the State's citizens, and a significant percentage of those individuals are likely to be deterred from voting." However, no doubt to the consternation of those who claim that election fraud is a myth, even Souter acknowledged the importance of "combating voter fraud." Justice Breyer wrote a separate dissent in which he made clear that he did not believe that a voter ID law was automatically unconstitutional, but he found the Indiana law to be a substantial burden on voters and therefore unconstitutional. Interestingly enough, he actually praised the voter ID laws implemented in Florida and Georgia as examples of "significantly less restrictive" laws that could still accomplish the goals of such a law, and he seemed particularly impressed with the very extensive education effort that Georgia went through to make sure that its voters were aware of the requirements of the new voter ID law and how to obtain free IDs.

While this decision was a substantial victory for proponents of voter ID, the balancing test used by Justice Stevens in the lead opinion guarantees that there will be more litigation filed over voter ID laws. Liberal organizations like the NAACP will continue to challenge such laws, arguing that they are unconstitutional as applied to specific voters. Such cases may be rather difficult to win, however. It is clear that at least three justices (Scalia, Alito and Thomas) are not open to the idea of facial challenges to voter ID laws based on the burden imposed on individual voters. Justices Stevens, Roberts and Kennedy found constitutional what is considered to be the most restrictive voter ID law in the country. And even Justice Breyer, while he did not like the Indiana law, spoke approvingly of other voter ID laws that have been strongly attacked by many liberals.

Beyond the legal issues involved, the *Crawford* case also revealed a fundamental philosophical conflict between two perspectives rooted in the machine politics of Chicago. Justice John Paul Stevens, who wrote the decision, grew up in Hyde Park, the city neighborhood where Senator Barack Obama— the most vociferous congressional critic of voter ID laws— now lives. Both men have seen how the Daley machine has governed the city for so many years, with a mix of patronage, contract favoritism and, where necessary, vote fraud. That fraud became nationally famous in 1960, when Mayor Richard J. Daley's extraordinary efforts swung Illinois into John F. Kennedy's column. In 1982, inspectors estimated as many as one in ten ballots cast in Chicago during that year's race for governor to be fraudulent for various reasons, including votes by the dead.

Justice Stevens witnessed all this as a lawyer, as special counsel to a commission rooting out corruption in state government, and as a judge. On the Supreme Court, this experience has made him very mindful of these abuses. In 1987, when the high court vacated the conviction of a Chicago judge who had used the mails to extort money, Justice Stevens wrote a stinging dissent, taking the rare step of reading it from the bench. The majority opinion, he noted, could rule out prosecutions of elected officials and their workers for using the mails to commit vote fraud. Three years later, Justice Stevens ordered Cook County officials to stop printing ballots that excluded a slate of black candidates who were challenging the Daley machine. The full court later ordered the black candidates back on the ballot.

Barack Obama has approached Chicago politics differently. He came to the city as a community organizer in the 1980s and quickly developed a name for himself as a litigator in voting cases. In 1995, Governor Jim Edgar, a Republican, refused to implement the federal "Motor Voter" law. Allowing voters to register with a postcard and blocking the state from culling voter rolls, he argued, could invite fraud. Obama sued on behalf of the Association of Community Organizations for Reform Now, and won.

ACORN's efforts to register voters have been scandal-prone in many states, as outlined in Chapter Three. Despite this record—and polls that show clear majorities of blacks and Hispanics supporting voter ID laws—Obama continues to back ACORN. They both joined briefs urging the Supreme Court to overturn Indiana's law.

Last year, Obama put on hold the nomination of Hans von Spakovsky for a seat on the Federal Election Commission. As a Justice Department official, von Spakovsky had supported a Georgia law requiring photo ID. In a letter to the Senate Rules Committee, Obama wrote that "Von Spakovsky's role in supporting the Department of Justice's quixotic efforts to attack voter fraud raises significant questions about his ability to interpret and apply the law in a fair manner." Of course, an even stricter law than the one in Georgia has now been upheld by the Supreme Court, removing Obama's chief objection.

The hold on the von Spakovsky nomination has left the Federal Election Commission with less than a quorum. As a result, the FEC cannot open new cases, hold public meetings, issue advisory opinions or approve John McCain's receipt of public funding for the general election. Now the Senate majority leader, Harry Reid, claims that filling the FEC's vacancies will take "several months" even without the hold on Hans von Spakovsky.

All this may be smart politics, but it is far removed from Obama's call for transcending the partisan divide. Then again, Obama's relationship to reform has always been tenuous. Jay Stewart, the executive director of the Chicago Better Government Association, notes that while Obama supported ethics reforms as a state senator, he has "been noticeably silent on the issue of corruption here in his home state, including at this point, mostly Democratic."

So we have the irony of two liberal icons in sharp disagreement over the Supreme Court's *Crawford* decision. Justice Stevens, the real reformer, believes that voter ID laws are justified to prevent fraud. Barack Obama, the faux reformer, hauls out discredited rhetoric that such laws disenfranchise voters.

ACORN's national political arm has endorsed Obama. And its "nonpartisan" voter registration affiliate has announced plans to register hundreds of thousands of voters before the November election—an election in which Obama is the Democratic candidate.

Seven

The Myths of Florida Live On

THE CURRENT TOXIC POLITICAL ATMOSPHERE, IN WHICH one side is concerned about vote fraud and the other about voter disenfranchisement, is largely the product of the elephant in the parlor left over from the 2000 election. Of course, I'm talking about the Florida recount, the gold standard for botched elections, and all the bitter recriminations it launched. The Florida battle returned to the news as the 2008 election approached. *Recount*, the Kevin Spacey movie about the debacle in Florida that will play endlessly on HBO between now and November, reminds us just how much of a political Rubicon the nation crossed in those thirty-six days of hanging chads and butterfly ballots. Should this fall's presidential race be close, platoons of lawyers stand ready to reprise the Florida nightmare—though probably in a different state and quite possibly in more than one.

Those hoping for a balanced account of the Florida 2000 battle certainly won't get it from HBO, which portrays a high-minded Gore team failing to match the ruthlessness of George W. Bush's advisers. The unspoken message is that Democrats will have to fight meaner and harder next time to avoid losing to the likes of James Baker, who served as Bush's strategist. Katherine Harris, Florida's Republican secretary of state in 2000, is portrayed by the actress Laura Dern as a vapid puppet of shadowy conservative forces. In interviews, Ms. Dern called her character "the villain of the piece."

There are little stabs at fairness, such as when a Bush attorney, Ben Ginsberg, is allowed a scene where he stares at his hotel television as Gore's campaign chairman, William M. Daley, demands that only selected counties be recounted. "His daddy stole it for JFK," an appalled Ginsberg shouts, referring to the late mayor Richard J. Daley of Chicago. "Now he's going to steal it for Gore."

The movie doesn't note the endless post-election recounts sponsored by various media outlets that found Bush would have won if all of Florida's votes had been recounted. But the main lesson from *Recount* is not a partisan one. As a sympathetic review in the *Los Angeles Times* noted, "events in Florida exposed so many overlapping and often incomprehensible flaws in the voting process that it is impossible to list them all. From the schoolyard mentality of party politics to the inconsistent voting regulations, from the arbitrary design of ballots to the possible corruption of the polling places, it's impossible not to wonder whether every state should have had a recount."

There are many issues to debate in the sordid Florida experience, but one of the most intriguing is how a cottage industry has sprung up among liberals to perpetuate what John Edwards, the Democratic vice presidential nominee in 2004, called "an incredible miscarriage of justice" in Florida. Jesse Jackson still refers to Florida as "the scene of the crime" where "we were disenfranchised. Our birthright stolen."

Such assertions are simply not supported by the facts. For example, in *Fahrenheit 9/11*, Michael Moore alleges that "under every scenario Gore would have won" Florida without the intervention by the United States Supreme Court. But in fact every single recount of the votes in Florida determined that George W. Bush had won the state's twenty-five electoral votes and therefore the presidency. The recounts included a manual count of votes in largely Democratic counties by a consortium of news organizations, among them the *Wall Street Journal*, the *Boston Globe*, the *Los Angeles Times* and CNN. As the *New York Times* reported on November 21, 2001, "A comprehensive review of the uncounted Florida ballots from last year's presidential election reveals that George W. Bush would have won even if the U.S. Supreme Court had allowed the statewide manual recount of the votes that the Florida Supreme Court had ordered to go forward." The *USA Today* recount team concluded: "Who would have won if Al Gore had gotten manual counts he requested in four counties? Answer: George W. Bush."

Why do liberals persist in propagating the Myth of the Stolen Election? Many of them sincerely believe in it, all this evidence notwithstanding. Others see it as a rallying cry that can bring out some of the Democratic Party's core voters.

The Florida controversy also offers a pretext for some to talk about other changes they want to make in election laws. The NAACP, for example, wants to "re-enfranchise" four million felons who have lost the right to vote because of their crimes. Some liberals would even like to extend voting privileges to noncitizens. In July 2004, the San Francisco Board of Supervisors voted to give noncitizens, legal or illegal, the right to vote in local school board elections; but San Francisco's famously radical voters rebelled, rejecting the idea in the November election. The idea of giving noncitizens a vote lives on, however. The ACLU has sued the U.S. attorney in San Francisco because he matched voting records against lists of legal immigrants who were not yet citizens. The ACLU argued that trying to determine whether noncitizens were voting would have a "chilling effect" on Hispanic voting.

The Republican establishment largely decided to ignore the Democrats' allegations of theft in Florida and move on. "People want their leaders to talk about the future," said the

GOP strategist Ralph Reed. "They don't want anger and pessimism and personal attacks."

But other party members say that Republicans can't simply let Michael Moore–style claims about the Florida recount go unchallenged. "I've had discussions with a number of friends and they say they're tired of repeating the same thing over and over," said Peter Kirsanow, a Republican member of the U.S. Commission on Civil Rights in 2004. "But that's what liberals do and that's why they're successful. They spread these myths until they're accepted as truth. Any sort of falsehood that drives people to vote one way needs to be corrected."

After all the media recounts of 2001 showed that George W. Bush would still have won under any fair standard, Democratic activists have narrowed their charges to the purported disenfranchisement of black voters. The Civil Rights Commission, led at the time by Mary Frances Berry, a Democrat, issued a scathing majority report in 2002 alleging "widespread voter disenfranchisement" and accusing Katherine Harris and Jeb Bush, Florida's governor, of "failing to fulfill their duties in a manner that would prevent this disenfranchisement." But when it comes to actual evidence of racial bias, the report draws inferences that are not supported by any data and ignores facts that challenge its conclusions.

Since we have a secret ballot in America, we do not know the race of the 180,000 voters (2.9 percent) of the total who voted in Florida whose ballots had no valid vote for president. Machine error cannot be a cause of discrimination since the machines do not know the race of the voter either, and in any case it accounts for about one error in 250,000 votes cast. (And as some have asked, is it not bordering on racism in the first place to assume that those who spoil ballots are necessarily minority voters?) One-third of the supposedly disenfranchised voters' ballots were "undervotes"—that is, ballots that showed no vote for president. Think for a moment about your own experience as a voter: have you ever declined to vote for some office on the ballot when you went to the polls? Studies show that over 70 percent of undervotes, where no candidate is selected, are cast deliberately by voters who prefer not to choose from the available options.

The Civil Rights Commission report also discusses "over-voting," the marking of more than one candidate for an office. Even chairman Mary Frances Berry admitted that she had sometimes "over voted unintentionally." In any case, voter error, whether intentional or inadvertent, is not the same thing as racial discrimination.

Nor, as a powerful dissenting report from commissioners Abigail Thernstrom and Russell Redenbaugh pointed out, was the commission able to come up with "a consistent, statistically significant relationship between the share of voters who were African-American and the ballot spoilage rate." John Lott, an economist and statistician from the Yale Law School, studied spoilage rates in Florida by county in the 1992, 1996 and 2000 presidential elections and compared them with demographic changes in county populations. He concluded that "the percent of voters in different race or ethnic categories is never statistically related to ballot spoilage."

Lott found that among the twenty-five Florida counties with the greatest rate of vote spoilage, twenty-four had Democratic election officials in charge of counting the votes. He concluded that "having Democratic officials in charge increases ballot spoilage rates significantly, but the effect is stronger when that official is an African-American." Commissioner Thernstrom argued that "it is very difficult to see any political motive that would lead Democratic local officials to try to keep the most faithful members of their party from the polls and to somehow spoil the ballots of those who did make it into the voting booth."

In fact, Florida 2000 was not a startling anomaly when it came to ballot spoilage. The rates across the country ranged between 2 and 3 percent of total ballots cast. Florida's rate in 2000 was 3 percent. In 1996 it was 2.5 percent. Glitches occur in every election—which is not to downplay the problem, but to put it into perspective. For example, the number of ruined ballots in Chicago alone was 125,000, compared with 174,000 for the entire state of Florida. Several states experienced voting problems remarkably similar to those in Florida. But the closeness of the 2000 election in the Sunshine State created a prime opportunity for racial demagoguery.

Doubtful Disenfranchisement

The Civil Rights Commission also focused on issues such as the state's decision to keep a list of felons who, according to Florida law, would be barred from voting. It claimed that this decision "has a disparate impact on African-Americans" since a higher percentage of blacks are convicted of felonies. That's true, but it's not a voter discrimination issue; it is an issue for the criminal justice system and the state legislature.

It is also true that the database of the names of felons set up for the state by Database Technologies, a private company, contained many errors. But the liberal-leaning *Palm Beach Post* found that "a review of state records, internal e-mails of [company] employees and testimony before the civil rights commission and an elections task force showed no evidence that minorities were specifically targeted." Indeed, the application of the law against felon voting in 2000 skewed somewhat the opposite way: whites were actually the most likely to be erroneously excluded from voter rolls. The error rate was 9.9 percent for whites, 8.7 percent for Hispanics, and only 5.1 percent for African Americans. Furthermore, the list wasn't created by Katherine Harris or any other Republican. A mandate for the list was passed into law in 1998, sponsored by two Democratic legislators and signed by a Democratic governor,

Lawton Chiles, Jeb Bush's predecessor. The law came about in response to the Miami mayoral election in 1997 that was over-turned by a court due to widespread fraud, with votes from disqualified felons and dead people. And Harris had no power to remove voters from the rolls. In Florida's decentralized election system, that is reserved for elected county supervisors of elections. The list merely served as a tool for them to use and verify with their own records.

Both the *Miami Herald* and the *Palm Beach Post* found that, if anything, county officials were too permissive in whom they allowed to vote, and this largely benefited Al Gore. An analysis by the *Post* found that 5,600 people whose names matched the names of convicted felons who should have been disqualified were permitted to cast ballots. "These illegal voters almost cer-tainly influenced the down-to-the-wire presidential election," the *Post* reported. "It's likely they benefited Democratic candi-date Al Gore. Of the likely felons identified by the Post, 68 per-cent were registered Democrats." Furthermore, the *Post* found no more than 108 "law-abiding" citizens of all races who "were purged from the voter rolls as suspected criminals, only to be cleared after the election." In fact, during all the various lawsuits against Florida, only two people testified that they were not allowed to vote because their names were mistakenly on the list. But in contrast to this trivial number, Bill Sammon, now with the *Washington Examiner*, points out that some 1,420 military ballots, many clearly received on or before Election Day, were disqualified at the behest of Democratic lawyers because they didn't technically comply with Florida's law requiring a foreign postmark. Sammon writes that this and the illegal votes from felons are "what-ifs" that "a truly fair and objective press" would discuss, but the establishment media does not because "they would only serve to reaffirm the legitimacy of Bush's victory."

Other charges from Democratic activists turned out to be "falsehoods and exaggerations," Sammon contends. For instance, when the commission investigated the charge that a police traffic checkpoint near a polling place had intimidated black voters, it turned out that the checkpoint operated for ninety minutes at a location two miles from the polling place and not even on the same road. And of the sixteen people given citations, twelve were white.

Time-Zone Turnout

In his film *Fahrenheit 9/11*, Michael Moore tried to demonize the FOX News Channel, claiming that because a cousin of George W. Bush, John Ellis, was working on the network's election desk that night, FOX gave the public the mistaken impression that Bush had won. The film shows CBS and CNN calling Florida for Gore, followed by a voiceover sneering, "Then something called the FOX News Channel called the election in favor of the other guy." But Moore leaves out the fact that FOX first called Florida for Gore—and didn't call it back until 2:16 A.M. Eastern. Indeed, all the networks, FOX included, helped Gore by prematurely calling the Florida polls as closed at 7:00 P.M. Eastern when in fact they were still open for another hour in the state's western Panhandle, which lies in the Central time zone and is heavily Republican. (CBS alone declared Florida's polls to be closed thirty-three times between 7:00 and 8:00 P.M. Eastern.) Then at 7:48, the networks, led by NBC, started calling the state for Gore while voters in the Panhandle still had twelve minutes to vote. Of the thousands of voters who were standing in line or en route and heard the news on radio, many gave up and went home.

"By prematurely declaring Gore the winner shortly before the polls had closed in Florida's conservative Panhandle, the media ended up suppressing the Republican vote," concluded John Lott. John McLaughlin, a Republican pollster, estimated that George W. Bush lost thousands of votes. His poll, conducted November 15 and 16, showed that the misinformation about poll hours and the premature calling of Florida for Gore dissuaded 28,050 voters from casting ballots; 64 percent of these would have voted for Bush. Even a study commissioned by the Democratic strategist Bob Beckel concluded that Bush suffered a net loss of up to 8,000 votes in the western Panhandle as a result of confusion sown by the networks.

While some caution should be brought to these polls because they were taken after the turnout in the Panhandle had become an issue and responses might reflect the political views of those surveyed, statistical evidence on voter participation rates implies a similar drop in voting. In an article in the academic journal *Public Choice*, Lott examined voter turnout rates for Florida counties from 1976 to 2000 and found a significant drop-off in turnout for the twenty western Panhandle counties relative to the rest of the state in 2000. The results suggest a net loss of 90,000 votes for Bush. Other evidence he examined on time-of-day turnout during the 2000 election found that the western Panhandle counties actually experienced a relatively high turnout during the first half of the day, but this slipped at the end of the day to slightly below the rest of the state. These data point to a net loss for Bush of between 7,500 and 10,000 votes.

Evaluating all these estimates is more than a mathematical exercise. In fact, Gore would have had much less moral authority to contest the Florida results had his margin of defeat been 10,000 votes. As Bill Sammon points out, "A five-digit margin would have been much more daunting for Gore to overcome than a three-digit one."

Palm Beach Mystery

Something strange happened in Palm Beach County on election night 2000. No, I'm not referring to the butterfly ballot that we all heard about *ad nauseam*. Nor am I going to discuss the unusually large 3,400 votes cast for Pat Buchanan in Palm Beach, many of them in predominantly Jewish and Democratic precincts, nor the hanging chads and dimples that entered our electoral lexicon as a result of what happened there.

In the confusion and chaos after the 2000 election, an anomaly occurred that many people believe ended up costing George W. Bush thousands of votes in Palm Beach. It appears that as many as 15,000 votes may have been altered and subtracted from the Bush total in Palm Beach County.

Bear with me while I go through some numbers; they are important because they suggest fraud. One former Democratic congressman I spoke with said that "no other conclusion explains the bizarre numbers"; and two law enforcement officers said they received credible reports on election night of tampering with punch-card ballots in Palm Beach, but in the chaos of the post-election period they were not told to follow up on the tips.

Palm Beach County has grown more Democratic over the years as the numbers of immigrants and elderly retirees from the Northeast have increased. The county voted for the first President Bush in 1988 but in 2000 it gave Al Gore a huge 62.3 percent of the vote, significantly higher than Bill Clinton's 58 percent in Palm Beach in 1996.

George W. Bush's 152,969 votes in Palm Beach in 2000 was such a weak showing that the losing Republican candidate for U.S. Senate, Bill McCollum, won both more votes (154,642) and a higher percentage of the vote in Palm Beach than Bush did, even though statewide McCollum lost by 284,000 votes (four percentage points) and Bush, as we know, came out ahead.

But what really got some Republicans and outside observers scratching their heads after the recount chaos subsided was the fact that George W. Bush had also been outpolled by the combined vote of the four Republicans running for Congress in Palm Beach, an even more unusual occurrence. Together, the Republican candidates won 158,211 votes in Palm Beach, edging out Bush's 152,969. By comparison, the total of the four Democratic candidates for Congress reflected the traditional drop-off in votes from the presidency to the U.S. House: the four Democrats won a total of 214,307 votes, considerably less than Al Gore's 269,732 votes.

There were other strange occurrences in Palm Beach on election night. Palm Beach County voters seemed uniquely incapable of understanding and using Votamatic punch-card ballots in such a way as to avoid overvoting, that is, voting for more than one candidate for the same office. Palm Beach produced 19,120 overvotes that night, a 4.4 percent error rate—almost ten times the error rate of 0.4 percent in the rest of Florida, or indeed of *any* other large jurisdiction in the country that used punch-card ballots other than Chicago.

Other counties used Votamatic punch-card systems on election night 2000 and did not have nearly the overvote problem that Palm Beach did. In Harris County (Houston), Texas, where almost a million votes were cast on Votamatic punch-card machines, there were only 6,500 (0.7 percent) overvotes and 14,690 (1.5 percent) undervotes (no votes) for president. San Diego County in California—a county with more seniors, minorities and new immigrants in its population mix than Palm Beach County—had an overvote rate of 0.5 percent. So, one should ask, why such a problem in Palm Beach, where overvoting approached 5 percent?

Only in Palm Beach County did Gore gain 750 votes in the initial post-election recount and Bush almost nothing. In 50 out of 67 Florida counties the total change was less than seven votes, and in 63 out of 67 counties the total change was less than thirty votes either way. Further, in 63 out of 67 counties the changes were somewhat evenly divided between all the candidates, in rough proportion to their original number of votes.

In *every* precinct in Palm Beach where Gore got more votes than there are registered Democrats, Bush received less than 60 percent of the registered Republican votes. In *no* precinct in Palm Beach did Bush win more than 80 percent of the number of registered Republicans overall. Indeed, Palm Beach County had the lowest rate of votes for Bush per registered Republican voter of any county in Florida and was in the lowest 10 percent in the country for counties with party registration.

There was certainly no lack of interest in the presidential race that year; it was expected to be close and Florida was a battleground state. Bush was a popular nominee in his own party. There were equally massive get-out-the-vote efforts by both parties. As shown by the absentee ballot numbers, there was equal interest in the election by both parties in Palm Beach. So why did George Bush do so poorly in Palm Beach relative to everywhere else in the state?

It is likely that some 15,000 Republicans went to the polls and something happened: Either they recoiled in disgust at their party's presidential candidate, or forgot to vote for him, or (and this is most likely) had their vote show up as a "double-punch" or overvote that was later thrown out. Some of the overvotes in Palm Beach County represented Gore voters who had also voted for Buchanan, but the 2003 recollections of some workers who recounted the Palm Beach ballots after Election Day indicated that far more ballots showed votes for both Gore and Bush.

Overvotes—where a ballot shows a vote for more than one candidate for an office—should concern us more than under-votes—where a ballot shows no vote for a particular office. Overvotes are often the result of human error, and efforts must be made to reduce the chances that they will be cast. But some overvotes may have a less benign explanation. Punch-card voting is particularly vulnerable to manipulation, especially if the ballots aren't counted at the precinct but instead must be transported by car to a central counting station.

I was told by two former law enforcement officers and a poll worker that they believe ballot tampering affected some Bush ballots on election night. This fraud took place after the polls had closed and the poll watchers had gone home. Precinct officials improperly reopened the ballot transfer cases, in at least one instance while taking the "scenic" route to the election center where the punch cards would be tabulated. Using a nail, pencil or other sharp device, they would take a ballot and punch out Al Gore's name for president. If the person had voted for Gore, the nail would go through air. But if the person had voted for George Bush or anyone else, the ballot would be invalidated, thereby reducing the vote count for that candidate. One former law enforcement officer told me that this tampering was done in at least two heavily Democratic precincts that registered an unusually low number of Bush votes.

Reducing your opponent's vote count is just as effective as adding new ballots for your candidate, and virtually undetectable. In the absence of whistleblowers, the only way to figure out if this kind of tampering occurred in Palm Beach County would be to examine the overvoted ballots for their two presidential choices, and then look at the preferences further down. Ballots with mostly Republican votes might be double-punched for Bush and Gore on the presidential line. A closer examination of those 19,000 overvote ballots in Palm Beach County could have uncovered the story.

The statistician John Lott and other observers, curious about the Palm Beach overvote numbers, urged the media teams recounting the Florida ballots in the summer of 2001 also to examine the Palm Beach ballots to see if the alleged mischief might have occurred. But the recount teams disregarded these requests. "They just couldn't be bothered," said Lott. "A great opportunity was lost."

Of course, such an examination would have been suggestive but hardly conclusive. Democrats would have claimed that the fact that more overvotes existed for Gore simply proved he got more votes than Bush in Palm Beach County. But if many ballots featured a vote for George Bush *and* a vote for Al Gore along with votes for mostly or all Republican candidates for other offices, a reasonable suspicion would be that someone had punched out Gore chads to invalidate Bush ballots.

One need only have watched the hand recounts in Broward County to see how brazen some election officials can be. And the zeal of local partisans makes some observers suspect there was hanky-panky in south Florida in 2000. Palm Beach County was one of the last counties in Florida to release its voting results, and Al Gore's strong showing there reduced Bush's lead from 50,000 votes statewide to less than 1,500 when Palm Beach finally came in well after midnight. It is very likely that after the polls closed and ballots were collected for counting, people would have known how close the race was and that every vote would indeed count—or not count if something was done to it.

National Democrats, aware of voting irregularities in Palm Beach County, hired a Texas telemarketing firm to make several thousand calls into Palm Beach County on Election Day to urge citizens to declare that they were "confused" by the butterfly ballot, and specifically to say they were "confused" between the Gore and Buchanan ballot positions. As many news reports have shown, and as Buchanan has acknowledged, many of the 3,000 votes cast for him in Palm Beach were the result of confusion. But more than 3,000 voters claimed subsequently to have been confused and voted for Buchanan, no doubt prompted by the telemarketing calls.

All this shows that Democrats at the national level were indeed extremely interested in the Palm Beach results *before* the polls closed and the ballots were counted. The calls went out before anyone other than election officials knew how many double-punched ballots existed, or which ballot choices for president were double-punched. If someone locally knew that Palm Beach County's vote would be critical for victory and knew from news reports that some people were claiming they had accidentally cast a vote for more than one presidential candidate, it is certainly possible that someone might have concluded that some additional creative overvoting wouldn't be detected and couldn't be proven.

Apparently we now will never know what caused the Mystery of the Missing Bush Ballots. But that's history. We do know enough about how much proven fraud or electoral incompetence there is in Florida and other states to pay more rigorous attention to it in the future. If we don't, I have no doubt that in another close election, perhaps in November 2008, it will be déjà vu all over again. There will be more ballot snafus and more questions about fraud and we will ask ourselves why we didn't address those potential problems when we had the time to take preventive action.

Eight

Mississippi Stealing

IN JULY 2007, A FEDERAL DISTRICT JUDGE FOUND DIRECT evidence that the political machine in Noxubee County, Mississippi, had discriminated against voters with the intent to infringe their rights and that "these abuses have been racially motivated."

Among the abuses catalogued by Judge Tom Lee were the paying of notaries public to visit voters and illegally mark their absentee ballots, manipulation of the registration rolls, importation of illegal candidates to run for county office, and publication of a list of voters, classified by race, who might have their ballots challenged. The judge criticized state political officials for being "remiss" in addressing the abuses. The U.S. Department of Justice, which sued Noxubee officials under the Voting Rights Act, has called conditions there "the most extreme case of racial exclusion seen by the [department's] Voting Section in decades."

Explosive stuff, so why haven't you heard about it? Because the Noxubee case doesn't fit the media stereotype for voting rights abuses. The local political machine is run by Ike Brown, a twice-convicted felon. Ike Brown is black, and the voters who were discriminated against were white.

Judge Lee concluded that Brown retained his power "by whatever means were necessary." According to the judge, Brown believed that "blacks, being the majority race in

Noxubee County, should hold all elected offices, to the exclusion of whites." (Whites are 30 percent of the county's 12,500 people, but only two of the 26 elected county officials.) Judge Lee also criticized top officials of the state Democratic Party for "failing to take action to rectify [Brown's] abuses."

Voting Rights Turnabout

Every summer a memorial service is held in Philadelphia, Mississippi, about fifty miles southwest of Noxubee, for three civil rights workers who were murdered while trying to register black voters during the "Freedom Summer" of 1964. Their deaths helped spur Congress to pass the Voting Rights Act of 1965, which swept away poll taxes and other impediments to black voting. Ever since then, a consistent media story line has been built around fears that the South's racist past will return to squash black political aspirations.

But the reality isn't so simple. While voter suppression by whites still goes on and must be curbed, so too does incompetence by election officials that calls into question the validity of elections, along with outright vote fraud. The right to vote includes the right not to have one's vote diluted by someone who shouldn't be voting, who votes twice, or who doesn't even exist. Yet mild measures to increase the integrity of the ballot box, such as photo ID laws or efforts to better police absentee ballots, are routinely attacked as attempts to restore Jim Crow voting procedures.

Just look at the coverage of the Justice Department's botched removal of seven U.S. attorneys. Congressional Democrats have gone into overdrive to prove the Justice Department canned them for their failure to pursue vote fraud cases, which it felt should be given a higher priority. The confirmation hearing for Hans von Spakovsky, a sitting member of the Federal Election Commission, has drawn bitter opposition because some former Justice Department officials make strained claims that he pushed for laws requiring voters to show a photo ID as a means to suppress black voter turnout. He is also accused of derailing two investigations into possible voter discrimination and causing enforcement of voting rights cases to plummet. In fact, the Bush administration filed thirty-five voting rights cases in its first five years, as opposed to only twenty-five by the Clinton administration in its last five years.

Critics of the Bush Justice Department complain that its priorities have shifted away from traditional voting rights enforcement and question if Justice should be filing "reverse discrimination" voting rights cases like Noxubee. Joseph Rich, the chief of Justice's voting section until he resigned in 2005 to join the liberal Lawyers Committee for Civil Rights, has said he thinks the Noxubee case had merit but wonders if it was "really a question of priority" for a department with limited resources. "The Civil Rights Division's core mission is to fight racial discrimination," Rich told the blog TPMMuckraker.com. "That doesn't seem to be happening in this administration."

The old civil rights establishment notes that the Bush administration has so far filed only two complaints on behalf of black voters, compared with eight filed by the Clinton administration during its last six years. Liberals remark that of the voting rights cases that the Bush administration has filed so far, seven have been on behalf of Hispanics. But Hispanics are now the largest minority in the country, and it's hardly surprising that more cases would arise involving a population that includes many new citizens unfamiliar with how to combat voter discrimination.

All the Boss's Men

In Noxubee County, Judge Lee's ruling shows that there was extensive evidence of vote fraud. More than 20 percent of the county's ballots were routinely cast by absentee voters, despite requirements that everyone have a valid excuse to obtain one. A major reason for their proliferation was that Ike Brown, in his capacity as head of the Noxubee County Democratic Executive Committee, would pay notaries public to complete absentee ballots for voters, sometimes without their knowledge or consent. According to Judge Lee, Brown and his allies then "put in place a nearly all black force of poll workers and managers, over whom they had effective influence and control, and who, under Brown's direction, ignored or rejected proper challenges to the ballots of black voters."

During the 2003 primary election, witnesses testified, Brown personally left the local sheriff's office (where he had set up shop across the hall from where ballots were counted) to tell poll workers to "count every vote, count them every one right now." Kevin Jones, the incumbent superintendent of education, who is black, confirmed that Brown told poll workers to count the votes and that they complied.

Brown also went through the absentee ballots in other precincts the night before the August 26 runoff and put Post-it notes on some ballots with instructions indicating they should be rejected. Judge Lee found that "witnesses who saw the yellow stickers maintained that every sticker seen was on the ballot of a white voter."

The boss left nothing to chance. Witnesses testified that on the day of the runoff, as voters cast ballots in person at polling stations, poll workers walked up unsolicited to black voters, "taking their ballots and marking them without consulting the voters." Terry Grassaree, the county's chief deputy sheriff, threatened Samuel Heard, a candidate for sheriff against Grassaree's boss, after Heard complained about illegal distribution of campaign literature at the polls. "I'll put your ass in jail," said Grassaree.

Brown sounded like Huey Long when he explained his actions. Libby Abrams, a poll watcher for Heard, testified that Brown told her: "This isn't Mississippi state law you're dealing with. This is Ike Brown's law." When Ms. Abrams responded that she planned to have four poll watchers on hand as votes were counted, Brown told her, "Fine, fine, have as many as you want. I'll send the police on around to arrest you."

Brown also published a list of 174 names of voters he claimed were illegally voting in Democratic primaries while they intended to support Republicans in the fall election, and suggested he would challenge them. He planned a crusade to "root out disloyal Democratic elected officials and voters," including Larry Tate, a black county supervisor who had angered Boss Brown by supporting Senator Thad Cochran and Representative Chip Pickering, both Republicans.

The defense that Brown mounted against all these charges was that he had acted legally and was motivated solely by a desire to elect Democrats. He called the Justice Department's lawsuit an example of "persecuting the victim" and noted the irony that after the white establishment had oppressed blacks for 135 years, federal officials had the "preposterous" effrontery to challenge blacks who had achieved political control of Noxubee County only a dozen years ago.

Judge Lee would have none of it. "If the same facts were presented to the court on behalf of the rights of black voters, this court would find that [the Voting Rights Act] was violated," he wrote. As part of his ruling, he gave lawyers on both sides thirty days to file briefs in the civil matter laying out how they would end the election abuses. Defendants who violated his order could face contempt of court and fines.

It's unclear how much Brown plans to comply. He isn't returning phone calls from reporters. He may not be intimidated by the prospect of fines, having served time in federal prison a decade ago for tax fraud. Last year he refused to sign a consent decree in which county officials promised not to harass or intimidate white voters, fill out absentee ballots for voters or coach them.

In the aftermath of Judge Lee's order, the knives began to come out for Ike Brown. Jeffrey Rupp, a former mayor of nearby Columbus, recalled that "Ike used to come visit me in city hall, and he would close the door and tell me how we were going to do things in Columbus, how we were going to redraw our district lines in Columbus. I wasn't intimidated by Ike Brown then, but I'm especially glad others finally aren't too."

After years of tolerating and even abetting Brown, a group of Democrats finally revolted. In early 2008, they joined together to recommend that Brown be denied his twenty-year seat on the state Democratic executive committee. At the Democratic state convention in June 2008, Brown fought to retain his seat but was voted down. Asked about his defeat, Brown said, "The Bible says it doesn't hurt you to part with anything you brought in the world with you."

Reform Comes Slowly—But It Comes

For months after Judge Lee's ruling, Democrats must have felt they were being asked to part with a great deal more. In his final folly, Brown in 2006 had pushed Democratic Party officials to file a lawsuit to block the practice of Republicans voting in the Democratic primary under Mississippi's open primary law. "They come over and vote in the Democratic primary and it's for the white candidates and then in the general election they run and vote for Republicans," complained Ellis Turnage, the attorney for the Democratic Party. The Democrats asserted that state law guarantees them the "freedom not to associate" with interlopers in their primary.

Judge Allen Pepper, a Clinton appointee recommended by Senator Trent Lott, agreed, but he handed the Democrats a Pyrrhic victory in district court by ordering the state to create closed primaries—and to require photo ID at the polls. Democrats who have long used incendiary rhetoric to block approval of a photo ID law are howling.

The irony of their complaint wasn't lost on Marty Wiseman, director of the Stennis Institute of Government at Mississippi State University. He noted that "Democrats, many of whom fought long and hard during the bad old days to open up Mississippi's closed political system, are attempting to make their own case for 'freedom not to associate.'" Secretary of State Eric Clark, a Democrat, said his party made a "serious mistake" in filing the lawsuit. "I believe in opening doors to voting and not in closing doors," he said.

Even though Judge Pepper's ruling calling for voter ID was overturned by the Fifth Circuit Court of Appeals in June 2008, it still had the salutary effect of focusing attention on the deplorable state of Mississippi's election records, which the Greenwood Commonwealth, the largest newspaper in the Delta, notes "still has people on the rolls from the 1960s who haven't voted in decades, yet federal rules make it almost impossible to purge their names." That, it noted, was an invitation to vote fraud and manipulation *à la* Ike Brown.

At the conclusion of his ruling in the Noxubee case, Judge Lee cited the ruling of the Fifth Circuit Court of Appeals in *Welch v. McKenzie*, a 1985 case in which the court held that "the right to vote includes the right to have one's ballot counted. This includes the right to not have one's ballot diluted by the casting of illegal ballots or weighting of one ballot more than another."

Half a century ago, the issues involved were literally black and white. Now they are murkier and more nuanced. Not all villains in voting rights cases are white. I've interviewed Democratic candidates from St. Louis to Detroit to Newark who acknowledge that many of our voting systems are so underfunded and sloppy as to invite either rampant incompetence or outright fraud. The Justice Department's victory in Noxubee County isn't a win for one race over another, it's a signal that some rethinking of old stereotypes is in order.

Nine

The Fraud That Made
Milwaukee Famous

O NE REASON THAT ELECTION IRREGULARITIES PERSIST IS
that many people can't even agree on what to call it.
Liberal groups insist on calling the practice *voter
fraud*, with the implication that the alleged chicanery is primarily limited to fraud committed by voters themselves impersonating someone else at the polls—something they rightly
suggest is not all that common. Conservatives tend to refer to
vote fraud, a broader term that includes not only impersonation fraud but many other forms of mischief. Even so, they
also sometimes downplay certain types of fraud. Many Republican lawmakers pay scant attention to the widespread misuse
of absentee and mail-in ballots because those forms of voting
are popular with their constituents.

The clashing opinions of what constitutes fraud and just
how widespread it is are not easily resolved and are endlessly
debated by academics, pundits and advocates. That's why it's
useful when a professional law enforcement agency goes to the
trouble of documenting just how pervasive the problem is and
what forms it takes.

In February 2008, the Milwaukee Police Department's Special Investigation Unit released a stunning report that should
silence skeptics who say vote fraud is not an issue in Wisconsin,
a critical swing state whose last two presidential elections were
decided by fewer than 12,000 votes. The investigators found

after an eighteen-month probe that in 2004 there had been an "illegal organized attempt to influence the outcome of an election in the state of Wisconsin." Among the problems it cited were ineligible voters casting ballots, felons not only voting but *working* at the polls, transient college students casting improper votes, and homeless voters possibly voting more than once. The report said the problem was compounded by incompetence resulting from abysmal record keeping and inadequately trained poll workers. One investigator, after examining Milwaukee's election system, was quoted as saying: "I know I voted in the election, but I can't be certain it counted." Examples of incompetence included the fact that between 4,600 and 5,300 more ballots were cast than voters who were recorded as having shown up at the polls in Milwaukee. More than 1,300 registration cards filled out at the polls were declared "un-enterable" or invalid by election officials.

The sloppiness was so bad it hampered and often prevented efforts to prosecute wrongdoers who committed fraud. The report cited statements by jurors in federal court trials of two men accused of double voting. One trial produced a "not guilty" verdict and the other a hung jury. In both cases, jurors said after the trials that although there appeared to be evidence that these individuals had voted more than once, mismanagement of the voting records by the Election Commission presented them with questions about the record system and they could not find guilt "beyond a reasonable doubt." In conclusion, the investigative report found that "The Milwaukee Election Commission, through their ineptitude, raised enough reasonable doubt to prevent any further criminal prosecution" of voting violators.

The Milwaukee Police Department's report minced no words about what should be done to prevent future scandals: the state should end its policy of allowing people to show up at the polls on Election Day, register to vote and then immediately cast a ballot. "If a verification period would be provided to the Election Commission before any Election, the majority of the problems detailed in this report would not have existed," the report found. It also called for all voters to show a government-issued ID at the polls to prove their eligibility.

The report directly implicated the John Kerry campaign and allied get-out-the-vote organizations in widespread illegal voting committed by their campaign workers, many of whom came from out-of-state. The most common method they used was to abuse the state's same-day voter registration law, which allowed anyone to show up at the polls, register and then cast a ballot. Local election officials who asked for proof of residence from these Kerry campaign staff members were often stymied when "other staff members who were registered voters vouched for them by corroborating their residency. More alarmingly, other staff members who were deputy registrars for this election simply registered these individuals as Milwaukee residents, bypassing Election officials altogether. The actions of the listed campaign and 527 staff members appear to be violations of State of Wisconsin law...."

The report went on at length to detail how these paid, professional workers violated the law. Case #4 was an attorney who had lived in Washington, D.C., since 1999 but came to Wisconsin to help with the campaign and voted using an address in Milwaukee. Case #6 involved another attorney who was living in England before the 2004 election. After coming to work on the Kerry campaign in Milwaukee, the person registered and voted in the 2004 election using a Milwaukee address. The owner of that address was interviewed by investigators and "stated that #6's sole purpose in coming to the state of Wisconsin was to work on the presidential campaign" and that the person returned to England after the election.

Nor did investigators believe that ignorance of the law led to the casting of illegal votes. "It is difficult for the investigators to believe that paid professional campaign staff members, who were tasked with assisting in the registration of new voters and the facilitation of those voters ... would not have had a working knowledge of the voter eligibility requirements," the report stated. "The belief of the investigators is that each of these persons had to commit multiple criminal acts in an effort to reach their ultimate goal of voting, showing that the act was a conscious, intentional effort to commit a crime.... Registering a person to vote that was known to be ineligible, registering to vote when ineligible and the actual process of then voting are all crimes under Wisconsin State Statutes."

Nor did the police report find the problem to be isolated. The two 527 groups it identified "placed thousands of staffers and volunteers in Wisconsin" and those involved in illegal voting "represent multiple levels of both the organizations, from upper management to the street level canvassers." Thus, the report found there was "a strong possibility that the discovery of these random staffers voting illegally is the proverbial 'tip of the iceberg' as it relates to an illegal organized attempt to influence the outcome" of the election.

The problem with Wisconsin's 2004 election was not just criminal activity but also the gross mismanagement by election officials that made it impossible to have any confidence in the "official" result. Investigators found that "two persons who had entered guilty pleas to misdemeanor charges of Election Fraud within one year of the November General Election also were employed as Election Inspectors" when voting took place on November 2, 2004. A total of eighteen convicted felons were sworn in as deputy registrars in 2004. Of the fifteen felons who listed a sponsoring organization, eight named ACORN as their sponsor. "In Wisconsin we have been told, ad nauseam, that 'every vote counts,'" the report noted. "What is most troubling is that each ineligible ballot accepted in effect cancels a legal vote cast by a Wisconsin state resident."

Liberal groups quickly disputed the Milwaukee Police Department's findings. DEMOS, a New York–based think tank, labeled the report "grossly flawed" and said that "years of investigation by federal, state and local authorities have turned up little evidence of voter fraud in Milwaukee elections." It called the criticism of same-day registration procedures "gratuitous attacks" and said any attempt to end the law would "strip Wisconsinites of their voting rights."

But the report disputed the contention by DEMOS that a lack of prosecutions for vote fraud meant that the problem didn't exist. The investigators believed that at least sixteen workers from all levels of the Kerry campaign and the two get-out-the vote groups "committed felony crimes." But no prosecutors chose to pursue them, the report noted. "Although the investigators do not agree with this decision, it is certainly understandable given the lack of confidence that all involved have with the accuracy and reliability of Election Commission records." In other words, once again a local election system is shown to be so flawed it's hard to prove where the fraud begins and the incompetence ends.

The incompetence took many forms. For example, the police report found that Milwaukee had no system to prevent felons, who are blocked from casting a ballot under Wisconsin law, from voting, due to the same-day registration system: It determined that at least 220 ineligible felons voted in 2004. Because it listed someone as ineligible only if it found an *exact* match between a voter and an ineligible felon, the report noted "there is a strong probability that the number of felons illegally voting in November 2004 is higher."

Milwaukee police also remarked that the city has a sad history of abusing homeless voters, with the most famous incident being the "Smokes for Votes" scandal in which a Park Avenue heiress flew in from New York in 2000 to offer cigarettes to the homeless if they voted for Al Gore. "The Milwaukee homeless vote has the potential to affect the outcome of a local election," the report stated. "This vote portability and the abject poverty that defines homelessness make these unfortunate individuals vulnerable to become the tools of voter fraud."

Then there are the many thousands of college students from other states who fill Wisconsin universities. Many are registered to vote in their home states and cast absentee ballots there. But Wisconsin's loose same-day registration law allows many to vote where they go to school also. Take Sandberg Hall on the campus of Marquette University. In the fall of 2004, just over 2,600 people lived there. But a total of 5,217 registered voters listed that dorm address as their residence. This meant that over 2,600 people who didn't live in the hall were registered there and able to vote from an address where they didn't reside.

The police investigators' report wasn't one-sided. It demolished some of the most common arguments made by Republican activists that there was rampant "double voting" by people who showed up at polling sites to vote in someone else's name. But it did point out just how easy it is in Wisconsin to do just that and not get caught:

> A simple change of spelling in any portion of the individual's name, a variation of the person's given name, or any change of a digit in the date of birth could conceal a number of multiple votes and/or registrations.... Michael A. Smith can become Mike Smith, M. A. Smith, or Mickey Smith, depending on the person reviewing the Same Day Registration card, and unless a specific allegation is made against one of these name variants, the new name would just be added to the overall database, in effect allowing all three variants to vote in subsequent elections.

The report found that absentee ballots were also ripe for abuse, noting the case of a voter who had moved to California before the 2004 election, but told an investigator that he voted in Milwaukee because his vote "would count" in Wisconsin. Investigators "discovered that the Election Commission certified Absentee Ballots that were submitted by voters using addresses that were not legal residences," including several who actually lived in Canada.

At the heart of Wisconsin's troubled elections is the system that allows anyone to register on Election Day and then vote in all subsequent elections without showing any ID. There is a weak ID requirement on the day of registration, which is easily circumvented by having another person "vouch" for your residence in the area. Such a safeguard is precious little protection. "A person residing in the 1700 block of W. Wells Street voted as an On-Site Registrant using an Illinois identification card.... The Milwaukee Election Commission employees allowed obviously ineligible voters to cast ballots in races that were contested."

When it came to recommendations for reform, the Milwaukee investigators were blunt. "The one thing that could eliminate a large percentage of fraud or the appearance of fraudulent voting in any given Election is the elimination of the On-Site or Same Day voter registration system," they concluded. They went on to suggest that voters present a photo ID to prove their eligibility to vote. Other forms of ID were frowned upon: "The inclusion of identification alternatives such as a credit card bill, library card, lease, etc., where no photo is provided, does not ensure that the person presenting these types of documents is in fact the person they are asserting to be."

As for absentee votes, the report recommended an earlier deadline for submitting such ballots so their validity could be determined. It also cited evidence that the large number of absentee ballots cast in the 2004 election had overwhelmed officials. "Many of these electors are recorded as having voted, but their ballots were never processed." The investigators recommended that state officials require the training of additional election inspectors to make sure all absentee ballots are actually counted.

Naturally, the Milwaukee Police Department's report was met with mixed reactions. Attorney General J. B. Van Hollen, a Republican, called the findings "extraordinarily troublesome" and embraced many of the report's recommendations. But Governor Jim Doyle, a Democrat, questioned the authority of the investigators to suggest reforms: "Our goal should try to be to make sure everybody in the state votes," he told reporters. "I'm not sure why the Milwaukee Police Department should be the one deciding what the voting policy is," ignoring the fact that the legislature always has the final say in what election laws will be.

Liberal pundits were even more scathing. "We understand the sleazy, political reasons Republicans want to make voting more difficult for anyone not wealthy and white," wrote Joel McNally, a columnist for the *Capital Times* in Madison, the state capital. Amazingly, he contended that the report found "no evidence of any organized vote fraud" and that, in any event, "vote fraud has been essentially eliminated by federal laws that would send any voter to prison for voting more than once, a risky act that would make no real difference in any election."

Once again, note the effort to circumscribe the definition of vote fraud to impersonation at the polls and then to belittle it as rarely ever happening. While the Milwaukee Police Department's task force looked only at the city of Milwaukee, its report makes clear that vote fraud takes many forms and that its existence is very difficult to uncover and often impossible to prosecute.

This makes it all the more disturbing that only weeks after the report was released, U.S. Senator Russ Feingold joined with fellow Democratic lawmakers from Minnesota to introduce federal legislation to require states to have same-day voter registration. He claimed that the system had worked well in Wisconsin for over thirty years. "By allowing people to register in person on Election Day, we can bring more people into the process, which only strengthens our democracy," he said.

Given such efforts, the Milwaukee report is a fire bell in the night, a warning to federal lawmakers as well as states that are considering liberalizing their absentee ballot rules or joining the six states that currently have a system allowing same-day registration.

The report demonstrates just how easily felons can illegally vote and how campaign workers who knowingly register others illegally can themselves vote in states where they are obviously ineligible. Finally, it remarks that the time to combat vote fraud is long before any suspect ballot is cast. Noting the dozens of examples cited in their report, the investigators commented that "any fraudulent voter activity, would not have been discovered until after the questioned ballot had been cast" and the election already decided for one candidate or another.

Ten

Florida with Rain: Seattle Chaos

J ASON OSGOOD IS A COMPUTER PROGRAMMER ON A MISSION. That's why he's running as a Democrat for secretary of state in his home state of Washington. He wants to avoid another election debacle like the one the state endured in its 2004 governor's race.

That year, the country dodged a repeat of the Bush-Gore Florida election fiasco only because George W. Bush's margin in the decisive state of Ohio was 119,000 votes. But the one out of fifty Americans who reside in Washington State lived through a Florida-style nightmare for months. In the latest example of why this country needs to clean up and clarify its sloppy election systems, Douglas firs substituted for palm trees as the backdrop. The 2004 chaos in the Pacific Northwest showed how most states are as unable to handle a photo-finish election as Florida was when the *Bush v. Gore* legal fight occurred in 2000.

In the Evergreen State, the photo-finish race and ensuing legal disputes involved the contest for governor between Christine Gregoire, the Democratic attorney general, and Dino Rossi, a Republican state senator. The race ended in a virtual tie, with Ms. Gregoire finally declared the winner by 129 votes out of over 2.9 million cast after three recounts that stretched over almost two months.

The lessons learned from the Gregoire-Rossi fiasco are valuable in assessing the kind of disputes that could spring up in 2008—especially with the growing use of absentee ballots, which were a major factor in Washington State.

Jason Osgood wants to make sure the lessons of 2004 aren't forgotten. Last year, he almost singlehandedly blocked the King County Council in Seattle from spending $345,000 on ballot-tracking technology—using unique barcodes on ballots that are linked to a voter's identification—because he felt it threatened the secrecy of the ballot. Instead, he wants a FedEx-style tracking system. "You can keep track of where things are. You don't know what's inside the package, but you know where it is."

Now he is challenging Sam Reed, the Republican secretary of state who was in office during the 2004 recount mess, on a nonpartisan platform. "I think that the Republicans have legitimate grievances, as well as the Democrats," he told the *Seattle Times*. "This is a nonpartisan issue. King County elections had problems with their procedures in 2004. They misplaced boxes of ballots and Sam Reed gave them a pass." Osgood opposes expansion of mail-in ballots, noting that the state had to endure controversial, error-prone recounts of both a 2000 U.S. Senate race and the 2004 governor's race because of the enormous number of labor-intensive mail-in votes that were cast.

Reed vociferously disagrees, noting that state law at the time allowed him to intervene in a county election system only if he was invited to do so by the county. He has a point, but he is on less solid ground in his zealous support for having almost all voters cast mail-in ballots. They proved to be the major reason the 2004 election is still such a bitter issue in the state, with a majority of voters believing the election was not conducted fairly.

The Storm Clouds Gather

Washington State's 2004 election nightmare began when Dino Rossi (Republican) wound up on election night the apparent winner over Christine Gregoire (Democrat) by about 3,000 votes.

The trouble first became clear when it was realized that not all ballots had been cast or counted by election night because so many absentee ballots had been dropped off at polling places or were still in the mail. The race wouldn't be settled by the ballots counted at the close of business that night. Washington allows absentee ballots—which will likely be used by 70 percent of the voters this year—to be counted as long as they are postmarked by Election Day. Thus everyone knew that the way late absentee and provisional votes (cast by people not on the registration rolls, and subject to later verification) were counted might wind up swinging the election.

That set off a legal fracas over hundreds of disputed ballots in heavily Democratic King County (Seattle). The fact that the biggest problems in the election were centered on King County was no surprise to many. It was the only one of Washington's counties where the election director was a political appointee of the partisan county executive. All the other counties independently elected their top election official, thus creating some accountability. In King County's case, the Democratic county executive, Ron Sims, had handpicked Dean Logan as his election administrator.

The first dispute in King County involved provisional ballots that hadn't been counted because either there was no signature on the ballot or there was no signature match between the provisional ballot and the voter registration on record with officials. Democrats demanded the names and addresses of those voters so they could contact them and correct the errors.

County officials responded that in requiring all fifty states to offer provisional ballots, Congress had stipulated that such votes remain private. Republican lawyers argued that having partisans scavenge for votes would increase the potential for fraud.

But Judge Dean Lum said such arguments weren't as important as the need to make sure every vote counted—an echo of Florida in 2000. A full ten days after the election, while absentee votes were still being counted, the superior court judge ordered election officials to give the names and addresses of the provisional voters to the Democratic Party. Judge Lum did express regret that the judiciary was being "whipsawed in the middle" of a bitter partisan dispute and asked to "micromanage an election." But then he proceeded to do precisely that by allowing partisan workers the opportunity to mine flawed ballots after the election, for the first time in the twenty years that Washington has used provisional ballots.

Democrats spent the next three days knocking on doors and speed-dialing voters. Ryan Bianchi, communications assistant for Christine Gregoire, made it clear how blatantly partisan the approach was. Democratic volunteers asked if voters had cast ballots for Ms. Gregoire. "If they say no, we just tell them to have a nice day," he told the *Seattle Times*. Only if they said yes did the Democrats ask if they wanted to make their ballots valid. Republicans played catch-up by belatedly using their own phone banks to call voters and identify ballots that might fall their way if made valid. In the end, Democrats turned in some 600 written oaths from provisional voters and Republicans about 200. Then two days before the original vote count was certified, King County announced it had 10,000 more absentee ballots than it had previously estimated.

All these votes helped narrow Rossi's eventual lead to 261 votes as the late absentee votes were finally counted and the results certified on November 17. At that point, the state began a mandatory machine recount of all ballots. But in King County the recount went beyond running the ballots through the counting machines. Officials there "enhanced" 710 votes that had been rejected by the machines, in some cases altering them with white-out or filling in the ovals on the optical scan ballots. Again, these additional ballots benefited Ms. Gregoire. In 38 of the state's 39 counties, a total of only 208 net votes were added to either Rossi or Gregoire in the recount. Then came King County, which represents 30 percent of the state's voters. Ms. Gregoire, who won 58 percent of the overall King County vote, harvested a net gain of 219 votes—more than the changes in the rest of the state for both candidates combined.

Such creative counting brought Rossi's lead down to 42 votes when the machine recount ended on November 24, a critical threshold to justify further recounts and litigation.

Democrats put up the $750,000 required to pay for a third recount, about one-third of which was raised from donations from the liberal group MoveOn.org and the John Kerry campaign. The recount they paid for would be conducted by hand, a process that most election observers, including those in charge of King County, view as less accurate than a machine count. Former governor Booth Gardner, a Democrat, told a press conference that he thought Ms. Gregoire should have conceded if the final recount margin had been 100 votes or more. But he felt the margin of 42 votes made a laborious hand recount appropriate.

But was it? A hand count certainly isn't more precise, as the spectacle of Florida's chad counting proved in 2000. "When you're talking about close to 900,000 pieces of paper, I think the machine count is going to be more accurate than a manual count," admitted Dean Logan, the elections director of King County and a Democrat. "Every time you have human judgment and frailty enter into the process it will change the result," agrees Bruce Chapman, a Republican who served as Washington's secretary of state before becoming director of the U.S. Census Bureau in the 1980s. In an interview, he told me a hand recount would likely result in acrimonious litigation that would see the courts intervene to settle the dispute. John Carlson, a Seattle talk-show host who was the GOP nominee for governor in 2000, worried that "this state's reputation for clean government may not survive the bitter struggle that appears about to begin."

"A Messy Process"

The hand count got under way in early December. It didn't take long for still more new ballots to be discovered. On December 7, more than a month after the election, King County said it had found 561 ballots that had been rejected because election workers initially couldn't locate the voter's original signature in their records.

That egregious snafu came to light only because a King County councilman, Larry Phillips (a Democrat), accidentally learned that his own absentee ballot hadn't been counted. "It's unfortunate that it occurred," was Logan's reaction. He acknowledged that his staff became aware of the error only after Phillips scanned a list of his local constituents whose absentee votes had been rejected.

"My eyes locked on my name," Phillips told the *Seattle Times*. "I was under the absolute impression [that] not only I voted, but followed the instructions correctly. If it can happen to the King County Council chairman, it can happen to anyone else."

A couple of days later, another 22 ballots were found hidden in voting machines that had been put into storage. None of these ballots had been stored in sealed and secured boxes.

Election officials are usually leery of counting votes that haven't been kept under constant lock and key.

Nonetheless, the Democrat-controlled King County Canvassing Board, by a vote of 2 to 1, rejected the Republican county prosecutor's advice not to count the 573 additional ballots. Then someone noticed that the list of disputed ballots did not include any voters whose names began with A or B. Another treasure hunt turned up 150 more votes that had been mistakenly put into storage. Then Stephanie Arend, a local judge in neighboring Pierce County, stepped in and blocked the counting of all 723 new ballots. She said state law clearly stipulated that a recount was supposed to count only those ballots already ruled valid, not add any more ballots to the mix.

On top of all this, the actual hand tabulation of the rest of the ballots in King County also saw a change in procedures midway through. Officials announced that they were overturning the policy of not counting ballots that had ovals filled in for both candidates ("overvotes") and now would send these ballots to the canvassing board for final review. Officials said this represented no change in the rules, but the fact is that ballots were then being treated differently according to what point in the recount they were examined.

Changing the rules made a difference. For example, on another 2 to 1 vote the canvassing board agreed to count a write-in vote for "Christine Rossi" as a vote for Ms. Gregoire. The dissenting board member, Dan Satterberg, acknowledged that the oval for Ms. Gregoire had been filled in but said the board had long held that "if a voter fills in an oval for a declared candidate and then *writes* a different name in the write-in line the vote is invalid."

The vote changes piled up so that by December 21, Ms. Gregorie took the lead by eight votes. Democrats promptly claimed victory. The next day, the state supreme court overturned the Pierce County judge and allowed King County to count the

573 ballots it had discovered weeks after the election. King County wound up counting 566 of them. Ms. Gregoire told cheering supporters, "The election process is working exactly as it should."

After King County finished tabulating its newly found ballots, Ms. Gregoire was declared the winner by 129 votes two days before Christmas. She praised the whole process as "a model for the rest of the nation and the world at large about how an election system, as close as this (race) is, can be done with the highest of quality."

That was too much even for some of the officials involved in the recount. A few days later, King County's election supervisor, Dean Logan, acknowledged that it had all been "a messy process." On January 17 he admitted he didn't know who had really won the election.

No kidding. During the two recounts, Logan's office discovered 566 "erroneously rejected" absentee ballots. Evidence surfaced that dead people had "exercised their right to vote." Documentation was presented that 900 felons in King County alone had illegally voted and that military ballots were sent out too late to be counted. More than 300 military personnel who were sent their absentee ballots too late to return them would sign affidavits saying they intended to vote for Dino Rossi. A total of 700 provisional ballots were fed into vote-counting machines before officials had determined their validity. In the four previous November elections, King County workers had never mishandled more than nine provisional ballots in a single election.

Slade Gorton, a Republican former state attorney general and U.S. senator, joined with six Republican members of the King County Council in calling for a Justice Department investigation of the county's handling of ballots. Records indicate that some election officials in King County knew the absentee ballot report they filed in November was inaccurate because there was evidence that at least 86 ballots had been misplaced. Ignoring the requirement that they count the number of ballots received, they instead simply added together the number counted and the number rejected.

"That's appalling," said Sam Reed, the Republican secretary of state who frequently was praised by Democrats for being evenhanded during the recount process. "You just don't do those things." Even the office of Ron Sims, the Democratic county executive, admitted that "an outside review is probably a good idea." GOP lawyers noted that two-thirds of all the new votes that had been discovered since Election Day were cast in King County precincts that Dino Rossi won. (Christine Gregoire won 70 percent of King County precincts.)

The errors by election officials in King County were compared to the antics of Inspector Clouseau, only clumsier. Nearly 2,000 more votes were counted in King County than the number of individual voters who appeared on the list of those who had cast a ballot. Other counties saw similar, albeit smaller, excess vote totals. Rossi was exasperated, telling reporters, "I don't think I'm going out on a limb by asking for every vote to have a voter."

King County officials finally admitted that at least 348 unverified provisional ballots were fed directly into vote-counting machines. "Did it happen? Yes. Unfortunately, that's part of the process in King County," elections superintendent Bill Huennekens told the *Seattle Times*. "It's a very human process, and in some cases that did happen." Dean Logan, Huennekens' boss, conceded the discrepancy between the number of ballots cast and the list of people who were recorded as voting, but said the differential of 2,000 votes "does not clearly indicate that the election would have turned out differently."

Are voters supposed to trust an election merely because it can't "clearly" be shown to have been hopelessly tainted?

Logan was certainly singing a different tune in January than he was on November 18, when he responded to charges of voting irregularities in an e-mail to colleagues that read in part: "Unfortunately, I have come to expect this kind of unsubstantiated crap. It's all too convenient, if not now fashionable, to stoop to this level when there is a close race."

Let's Try Again

On January 7, ten days before the scheduled inauguration of the new governor, the Washington State Republican Party announced it would contest the election. A trial before Judge John Bridges was set for May 23 in the central Washington town of Wenatchee. Republicans said they were seeking a rerun of the election. Former secretary of state Ralph Munro, a moderate Republican, says that confidence in the election system had been so damaged that the only way to restore it was to consider holding a new election in February. He noted that King County had added ballots into its count so many times that almost no one other than the lawyers involved could easily explain the chain of events.

The Republican legal team compiled a strong body of evidence showing irregularities, certainly far more detailed than the evidence that North Carolina officials used early in 2005 to order a statewide March revote of the race for agriculture commissioner after a computer ate 4,438 ballots in a GOP-leaning county. Without those votes, the GOP candidate was leading by 2,287 votes out of 3.5 million cast. The Republican eventually won the rerun election.

A Strategic Vision poll of Washington voters taken in late January found that 53 percent of respondents favored a revote for governor; 35 percent opposed it; and 12 percent were undecided. If there was a revote, 51 percent said they would support the Republican, Dino Rossi; 43 percent would support

Christine Gregoire; and 6 percent were undecided. When asked who they believed actually won the gubernatorial election in November, 53 percent said Dino Rossi; 37 percent said Christine Gregoire; and 10 percent were undecided.

There was no provision in Washington state law for holding a new election. It would have to be ordered by the state supreme court or by a special session of the state legislature. Sam Reed, the secretary of state, said a rerun of the election was eminently doable given the precedent of a small town in Washington rerunning an election after it was discovered that some people who were ineligible had been allowed to cast ballots.

There was also a precedent for a statewide rerun of an election. In New Hampshire in 1974, John Durkin, a Democrat, ran for the U.S. Senate and very narrowly lost. A recount overturned the original result and gave Durkin a ten-vote lead over his Republican opponent, Louis Wyman. But then the state's Ballot Law Commission recounted the ballots and certified Wyman the winner by two votes. Durkin had no real evidence of fraud, but he contested the election anyway. The Democrat-controlled Senate sided with him and refused to honor the state's certification. The seat remained vacant for seven months. The debate in the Senate spanned one hundred hours over a month, with thirty-five inconclusive roll-call votes. The impasse ended only when Durkin agreed to a special election. He won that race, but then lost a bid for a second term in 1980.

In 2004, however, Gregoire and her fellow Democrats stood firm against the idea of an election rerun, calling it "absolutely ludicrous."

Slade Gorton responded that there was ample reason for a court to order a revote, saying, "No one can govern effectively under the cloud this race has created." He noted that state law doesn't require any showing of fraud to contest an election.

"That is irrelevant to whether the election should be done over," he says. "The law is quite clear in giving a court the right to void any election where the number of illegal or mistaken votes exceeds the margin of victory, and it has done so in the past."

Gorton noted that Secretary Reed had issued a report in 2003 saying that King County's sloppy election procedures could lead to just this sort of meltdown. "The county is not consistent in their ballot enhancement procedures," Reed's report concluded. "Ballot enhancement, while done in full view of political observers, does not use the procedures outlined in the Washington Administrative Code. Inconsistencies in how this procedure is handled significantly increase the possibility of a successful election [challenge to the results]." How prescient.

More Votes Than Voters

As depositions were taken before the May trial, more disturbing evidence of King County's conduct of the election turned up. Much of the evidence uncovered on the county's flouting of election laws first appeared on SoundPolitics.com, a blog run by Stefan Sharkansky. A computer consultant and a former liberal, Sharkansky calls himself a "9/11 conservative mugged by reality." He used his knowledge of statistics and probability to illustrate how unlikely some of the reported vote-count changes were. He and a group of dedicated volunteers pored through voting records after the lawsuit to overturn the gubernatorial election failed. Their effort was akin to what many national media outlets like the *New York Times* and the *Wall Street Journal* did in 2000 to see if they could figure out who would have won a recount in Florida.

"My goal was to figure out how King County managed to count so many more votes than voters, which nobody had managed to explain even during the trial," Sharkansky says. "We found that there really were hundreds of votes that were unlawfully accepted and we obtained photographs of the ballots from county records as proof." To this day, Sharkansky has many pairs of photos of absentee ballot envelopes showing when someone returned two absentee ballots and both were counted; many pairs of photos where someone cast both an absentee ballot and a provisional ballot and both were counted; and many photos of provisional ballot envelopes that were cast by someone who was not a registered voter but the ballot was tabulated anyway. In some of these cases the envelopes even had canvasser notes saying "Not registered, do not count."

Sharkansky also uncovered the fact that 527 of the 763 registered voters, or 70 percent, in Precinct 1823 in downtown Seattle used 500 Fourth Avenue—the King County administration building—as their residential address. A full 61 percent of the precinct's voters had registered only in the last year, and nearly all of them "live" at 500 Fourth Avenue. By contrast, only 13 percent of all King County voters registered in 2004.

Not all the voters at the county building are homeless or hard to find. Betty Fletcher, a noted local judge, and her husband have been registered at the county building for years. When I called her to ask why, she became flustered and said it was because of security concerns, specifically because "the Mexican mafia are out to get me." When I pointed out that her home address and phone number were easily found on the Internet and in property records, and asked whether she had improperly voted for state legislative candidates who would represent the county building but not her residence, she refused to answer and ended the conversation.

Judge Fletcher and her husband later reregistered at their proper address after their registrations were challenged. One of the few sensible reforms enacted by Washington's Democratic legislature after the 2004 debacle did end the practice of registering the homeless at public buildings. Even the homeless now have to provide a proper residence location, even if it's just the location of, say, the highway overpass that they sleep under.

Liberal officeholders in Seattle privately acknowledged that the combination of bloggers, talk radio and local think tanks like the Evergreen Freedom Foundation helped skeptics of the election's validity win the public relations war. Bob Williams, president of Evergreen, says his group wasn't focused on overturning Christine Gregoire's election so much as on highlighting the obvious problems in the vote count that cried out for permanent legislative fixes.

Joni Balter, a columnist for the *Seattle Times*, complained that the attack on the vote count by media outlets was "by now a near-military operation—air, land and sea." She blamed the radio hosts Kirby Wilbur, John Carlson and Mike Siegel for keeping listeners updated and in a constant state of outrage. "There's a lot to be outraged about," responded Carlson. "Last week, I did 13 out of my show's 15 hours on the election and people wanted more."

And the material kept coming. On April Fool's Day, Sharkansky posted a joke item about King County finding more ballots for Gregoire. Eerily, later that same day, King County disclosed (no joke) that it had found several dozen mail-in ballots that hadn't been counted!

The discovery of uncounted mail-in ballots sheds new light on the "Mail Ballot Report," which election staff had presented to the canvassing board prior to certification, purporting to show that all mail-in ballots were properly accounted for. The report didn't indicate that there were any missing uncounted ballots of the type that were just discovered. This omission reveals that the Mail Ballot Report was bogus. King County admitted that the Mail Ballot Report was "so flawed it was virtually meaningless." Later, King County's mail ballot manager, Nicole Way, said in a deposition that she and Garth Fell, assistant elections superintendent, agreed to the misleading report because officials didn't know how many absentee ballots were returned by voters.

These latest disclosures forced the King County executive, Ron Sims, to form an "Independent Election Review Panel" to advise him on election reforms. But he handpicked the members, and it was chaired by a major Democratic donor.

Separately, U.S. attorney John McKay responded to public calls for federal investigation into the election by effectively washing his hands of the matter: "As the Governor's race is a state election, concerned citizens who have information they believe is important to the electoral process should provide that information to state officials." He said it wasn't important that a federal presidential election had been conducted in the state at the same time as the governor's race.

The Court Looks the Other Way

The trial of the contested election lawsuit opened on May 23. The Republicans focused on the illegal votes—felons and others—and on the discrepancy between ballots counted and voters credited as evidence of impropriety. They argued for the use of proportional deduction to adjust each candidate's total (subtract the illegal or unexplained votes in each precinct in proportion to the share of each candidate's total in that precinct). This method is not contemplated in Washington state law but is used in some other states and by the U.S. House of Representatives in election contests. The Democrats argued that there was no evidence that the discrepancy between votes and voters was caused by anything other than clerical errors in crediting voters and no evidence that those were not valid votes.

Expert witnesses for the Democrats (two statisticians from the University of Washington) argued that there was no scientific validity to the proportional deduction method for determining the share of the illegal votes.

The judge ruled that there were 1,678 illegal votes cast (itemized by felons, double voters, etc.), and that there were 875 more votes than credited voters in King County and a total of 540 more uncredited votes across the other counties.

But the judge ultimately agreed with the Democrats that there was no evidence to attribute the uncredited ballots to illegal voting, and he accepted the Democrats' scientific argument against the proportional deduction method. His standard was that a ballot couldn't be subtracted from a candidate's total unless it could be proven for whom the vote was cast. The only adjustment he made to the vote total was to subtract the votes of four felons produced by the Democrats as witnesses who testified that they voted for Rossi. He thus widened Ms. Gregoire's official margin of victory from 129 to 133.

The state contest statute puts all the burden on the challenger, while the election officials (especially in King County) managed to sandbag discovery and prevent evidence of some of the most serious "errors" from being disclosed (such as the counting of multiple double votes and the counting of provisional ballots from unregistered voters).

Curiously, the failure of the Rossi lawsuit didn't make much difference in public opinion. A poll of state voters showed that more people believed that Rossi was the legitimate winner of the election *after* the trial than before. One reason may be that the trial never resolved the mystery of why there were more votes than voters in King County.

Was there fraud involved in the election meltdown? No judge ever established there had been fraud in the formal sense. Certainly there were individual voters who knew they were doing wrong by voting more than once or voting in the names of deceased persons. (A handful were prosecuted.) There were presumably many more voters who violated the rules without much thought, or who cast multiple ballots for innocent reasons such as forgetting they had voted absentee weeks earlier. Election administration systems failed to toss many of the duplicate votes.

There was also a disturbing incident at a nursing home in Lynnwood, north of Seattle. It appears that some elderly residents with dementia, or in one case someone who had been legally disenfranchised for incapacity, had ballots filled out for them by nursing home workers. Authorities were notified of the incident but no formal investigation was ever conducted.

Stefan Sharkansky, the blogger who has conducted an exhaustive investigation of the 2004 election, says, "I certainly think there was a kind of fraud whereby election administrators, primarily to protect their own jobs and reputations, intentionally deceived the public by failing to disclose and/or covering up errors and mistakes, and pretending that the election was more accurate than it really was." In other words, the manifest incompetence of election officials combined with the desire to cover it up resulted in a flawed election that voters could not have confidence in.

Sharkansky believes that King County officials created a porous system allowing votes to be counted without integrity checks. They were diligent about disclosing and correcting errors (like the rejection of the Larry Phillips ballots) that wrongly prevented ballots from being counted, but careful not to disclose errors where ineligible ballots were wrongly counted.

A Step Forward, a Step Backward

You'd think the Democratic legislature would be appalled at the rampant mistakes and move to fix them. Indeed, separate election reform packages passed by both the state house of representatives and the state senate contained such good ideas as changing the appearance of provisional ballots so they aren't as easily mixed in with regular ballots. The legislature also gave the secretary of state some new tools to clean up the voter rolls.

In 2007 and early 2008, more than 400,000 names were removed from Washington's voting rolls following the creation of the state's first integrated database system, including all of the state's 3.2 million voters from all 39 counties. The purged names included 39,814 duplicate voter registrations, 40,105 deceased voters, 4,500 improperly registered felons and over 210,000 inactive voters or those who had moved out of the state. "We really are improving the integrity of the system itself," says Sam Reed, the secretary of state.

All well and good, but Reed's actions may be overshadowed by another measure the legislature enacted, this one creating a universal vote-by-mail system similar to those in neighboring Oregon. Washington State's widespread use of mail-in ballots provided an excuse for Kathy Haigh, chairman of the committee overseeing election laws in the state house of representatives, to strip the election reform bill of a requirement that voters show photo ID at the polls. "Sixty-eight percent of the people are voting by mail," she explained. "When do they have to show ID? They don't, they have to sign." Precisely, replied her critics, which they cited as a reason that expanding mail-in elections would only increase the potential for fraud.

Universal vote-by-mail has now been instituted in almost every county for the 2008 election. But not in King County (no surprise there). Officials there tried to institute vote-by-mail in time for the 2008 election, but after they spent hundreds of thousands of dollars on it, the plan fell apart because it would have depended on uncertified equipment. It's no wonder that election reformers have developed a kind of gallows humor over how Washington, once renowned for its clean government, now finds its election system compared to those in Louisiana or Philadelphia.

That's why voters have taken matters into their own hands where they can. In November 2007, King County voters overwhelmingly approved I-25, an initiative to make the director of elections be an independently elected official (as in all the other counties in the state), rather than an appointee of the county executive. The Democrats on the county council dug in their heels to keep the elections office under the control of the Democratic executive for the 2008 election cycle, and engineered it so that the voters have to approve the initiative a second time in November 2008 and if again successful will choose the elections director in February 2009. As of this writing, no candidates have stepped forward.

Where Are the Players Now?

Leading characters responsible for the 2008 election meltdown seemed to land largely on their feet. Dean Logan remained a figure of ridicule until he resigned in June 2006 to become deputy voter registrar in Los Angeles County, which has as many people as the entire state of Washington. Last year he became the voter registrar in charge of all the county's elections. Talk about the Peter Principle at work.

Nicole Way, King County's mail ballot manager, was fired for failing in her duties by overlooking several dozen uncounted ballots that weren't discovered until March after the election. An arbitrator had her reinstated in her job, with back pay.

Garth Fell, Way's boss and collaborator in the falsified Mail Ballot Report, is now superintendent of elections in Snohomish County, just north of King County.

Bill Huennekens was demoted from superintendent of elections but kept on the payroll in special projects, and was placed in charge of King County's ultimately unsuccessful transition to all-mail voting.

John McKay eventually became one of seven U.S. attorneys who were replaced by the Justice Department in December 2006. McKay allies contended that he was let go in part because he resisted political pressure to conduct a full-scale investigation into Washington's 2004 gubernatorial election.

McKay claims he undertook a thorough investigation and found "no evidence" of crimes. He insists that he left "no stone unturned" in pursuing allegations of fraud in the governor's race and found no evidence of a crime. But in an interview with Stefan Sharkansky of SoundPolitics.com in May 2007, McKay admitted that he "didn't like the way the election was handled" and that it had "smelled really, really bad." His decision not to prosecute was apparently based on the threshold of evidence he insisted be met before he would even deploy FBI agents to investigate: a firsthand account of a conspiracy to alter the outcome of the election.

But McKay is incorrect in saying that he had to find a conspiracy in order to reach the federal threshold for election crimes. In Milwaukee after the 2004 election, U.S. attorney Steve Biskupic investigated many of the same problems as were found in Seattle: felons voting, double voting, more votes cast than signatures in poll books. In 2005, Biskupic concluded that he had found nothing that "has shown a plot to try to tip an election," but he nonetheless prosecuted and won six convictions for felon voting and double voting.

To his credit, McKay invited SoundPolitics.com to request his "close out" memo to the Justice Department on his decision-making process to clarify any remaining questions. In March 2008, a Freedom of Information Act request for his memo by Jonathan Bechtle, an attorney with the Evergreen

Freedom Foundation, finally brought the document to light. Throughout the memo, McKay made clear that he didn't want to probe the Washington governor's race: "After an extensive review of the applicable law, however, I concluded that even if the affidavits had been forged, because the federal issues on the ballot had already been decided by mid-November and because the conduct did not involve state action, the federal government did not have jurisdiction over the alleged conduct." In other words, there was never any chance the federal prosecutor would ever have gotten involved in the Washington meltdown.

ACORN Squashed

An interesting postscript to the 2004 governor's race surfaced in 2007 when felony charges were filed against seven ACORN workers for filling out false registration cards. Prosecutors said at the time that ACORN's oversight of its workers was virtually nonexistent. To avoid prosecution itself, ACORN agreed to pay $25,000 in restitution. Six of the seven workers pleaded guilty to felony fraud. The seventh is a fugitive.

Tom McCabe, executive vice president of the Building Industry Association in Washington State, says he is pleased that the evidence his group compiled on ACORN's activities was helpful in securing the guilty pleas of the workers. But he can't help but wonder if the ACORN workers who forged registrations in 2007 were part of the cadre of election workers who were allowed by a local judge to seek out voters who had given problematic signatures on their voter registration cards and help them "revise" their registrations in order to make their votes valid in the 2004 governor's election. "We may never know whether ACORN workers forged signatures in 2004, but we know they did in 2006," he says. "Those who think voter fraud isn't an ongoing problem should come to Washington State."

Dino Rossi is running for governor again in 2008—a rematch against Christine Gregoire. The latest polls show the race will be very close. Here's hoping the state can avoid another train wreck if the election is skin-tight close again.

Eleven

Politically Active after Death

S T. LOUIS IS KNOWN FOR ITS GATEWAY ARCH, ANHEUSER-
Busch beer and the magnificent Forest Park. But it has
also become infamous for having one of the worst-run
election systems in the country, a distinction which is of more
than local concern since Missouri is always a hotly contested
swing state in presidential and Senate elections.

St. Louis's rancid elections have become a civic black eye
and also a source of much rueful local humor. The columnist
Steve Hilton suggested that the city make lemonade out of
lemons and promote its ballot follies as part of a tourism
package:

> Hey, stay for the election. It's when dead people vote, and felons.
> The kids? They're sure to love Ritzy the Dog, who's proudly
> registered to vote. Don't miss Circuit Court. That's where you
> get a ballot after saying "I was sick." See a deceased person who
> needs more time to vote. St. Louis, where we vote past closing
> time.

The gallows humor acknowledges the fact that if Florida
had not dominated all the headlines after the 2000 election
and if Missouri had been a little closer, the nation's attention
might have been riveted on St. Louis, where abandoned voting machines, unguarded ballot boxes, confusion over poll

closing times, and a suspicious phone-bank message by Jesse Jackson threw the entire city's election into chaos.

On Election Day 2000, Gore-Lieberman campaign lawyers filed a suit swearing under oath that their plaintiff, one Robert Odom, was about to be denied his constitutional right to vote because of the times when the polls would be open. The lawsuit became the basis for circuit judge Evelyn Baker's order that the polls be kept open three hours longer in heavily Democratic St. Louis than in the rest of the state. The Missouri Court of Appeals later overruled her, saying that her order "would only permit voting by persons not entitled to participate"; and in that extra time allotted, the court later concluded, "it is probably impossible to know how many voters were improperly permitted to cast a ballot after the polls should legally have been closed." U.S. Senator Kit Bond (GOP) was exaggerating only slightly when he called Election Day in St. Louis "a major criminal enterprise designed to defraud voters."

The story begins the day before the election of November 7, 2000, when William Lacy Clay, the Democratic candidate for Congress running to succeed his father, the retiring incumbent Bill Clay, attended a Gore-Lieberman rally at the America's Center in St. Louis. In his speech to the crowd, the junior Clay said it was his intention to have the polls held open beyond the legal closing time. The next morning's edition of the *St. Louis Post-Dispatch* quoted him as saying, "If it [getting out the African American vote] requires leaving the polls open a little longer, we are going to get a court order to do it." The next day, both parties worked hard to bring out their base voters, knowing the state was a crucial battleground in the presidential race. George W. Bush and all the other Republicans on the ballot were in the fights of their lives. The governor of Missouri and Democratic Senate candidate, Mel Carnahan, was killed three weeks before the election but his name remained on the ballot. Carnahan's lame-duck successor promised to appoint the late governor's wife, Jean, if the dead man was elected over the incumbent Republican senator, John Ashcroft. In the end, the late governor beat Ashcroft by 49,000 votes, or 51 percent to 49 percent. Meanwhile, in the race for governor, U.S. Representative Jim Talent was defeated by Bob Holden, the Democratic state treasurer, by just 21,000 votes, or less than 1 percent. (No one knows exactly how much of a role fraud played in these results, but the Missouri secretary of state later found that 56,000 St. Louis–area voters held multiple voter registrations.)

With all these races in the balance, the pressure to get more voters to the polls became intense. At 3:20 P.M., the Gore-Lieberman campaign, the Democratic Party and Mr. Clay filed suit. The only party named in the suit that was not a candidate or a campaign organization was a mysterious figure named "Robert D. Odom." The suit contended that Mr. Odom had "not been able to vote and fears he will not be able to vote because of long lines at the polling places and machine breakdowns that have lasted for several hours." The lawyers filing the suit swore to its validity and their representations about Mr. Odom when they filed. They also alleged that up to 33,000 registered voters had been put on the city's list of inactive voters, leading to further delays if any of them tried to prove they were eligible to vote.

The case was originally scheduled to be heard by circuit judge Robert Dirker, but the lawyers for Gore-Lieberman used their right to ask for another judge to preside over the case. That would normally have meant another judge in Dirker's division, but instead the case mysteriously ended up in the courtroom of Judge Evelyn Baker, who sat on the juvenile court hearing cases involving miscreant minors.

Not that Judge Baker didn't have some experience with elections. Back in 1989, she had rejected an official request from the St. Louis Board of Election Commissioners to delay a primary after eleven inches of snow paralyzed the city. The election went on as scheduled, with abysmal turnout as hundreds of thousands of voters stayed home. But while she had been hardhearted in the past, this time she was filled with concern for those like Mr. Odom who were being prevented from voting. "I feel very strongly that people should be able to exercise their right to vote," she told the *St. Louis Post-Dispatch* in a post-election interview.

Attorneys for the election board pointed out that by law, any eligible voter in line at the polls at the closing time of 7:00 P.M. must be allowed to vote. When the board moved to have the suit dismissed, the lawyers for Gore-Lieberman insisted that Mr. Odom needed relief. "Mr. Odom is here and prepared to testify he was denied his right to vote based on the allegations in the petition," said Douglas Dowd, one of the lawyers.

Judge Baker never asked to hear from Odom, which was a good thing for the Gore-Lieberman lawyers because he couldn't have been in the courtroom. Kevin Cosh, the director of the St. Louis Board of Elections, found no person named Robert D. Odom registered to vote in the city. A Robert Odom had been registered to vote at 1414 Benton Street, but his registration had been cancelled after his death in 1999. In St. Louis, however, there is something of a tradition for the dead to remain involved in civic affairs.

At 6:30 P.M., after a cursory hearing to weigh Odom's complaint, Judge Baker ordered that the city's polls remain open until 10:00 P.M., three hours later than allowed by law. She ordered the downtown office of the election board to remain open for voting until midnight. According to an affidavit filed by Joshua Henning, sometime between 6:30 and 7:00, a prerecorded phone message from Jesse Jackson was sent out. All over St. Louis, residents picked up their phones and heard:

This is Reverend Jesse Jackson. Tonight the polls in St. Louis are staying open late until 10 P.M. in your neighborhood and until midnight downtown. Until 10 P.M. in your neighborhood and midnight downtown, at the Board of Elections. Keep the faith. Vote with a passion. Keep hope alive.

A similar, apparently coordinated effort was made by Vice President Al Gore to encourage voters to go to the polls after the legal closing hour. KMOX and KDNL radio stations each received a phone call from Gore between 7:00 and 7:30. Gore urged the station hosts to broadcast a message from him encouraging people to vote. Given the limited time between Judge Baker's order being issued and the Jackson and Gore interventions, it is difficult not to assume that their roles were arranged well in advance.

Judge Baker's decision was clearly at odds with state law. The Bush-Cheney campaign filed an emergency appeal and a state court of appeals quashed Baker's order at 7:45. The new order required that polls be closed at 8:15. However, locals report that voting in some precincts continued after 10:00. At 7:00, judges at 29 of the city's nearly 400 precincts walked away from their posts, exhausted after a fourteen-hour day, leaving ballot boxes unattended or in the care of a building custodian. The next day, St. Louis police found an abandoned voting machine in a vacant lot in the 3900 block of Olive Boulevard.

The tangle of events raised a host of questions, especially given that on Election Day the Gore-Lieberman campaign also filed an identical lawsuit (this time with a real plaintiff) seeking an extension of voting hours across the state in Kansas City. This suit was badly proofread, however, and in several places it referred to the individual plaintiff as "he/she," as if the sex of the voter allegedly denied the right to vote had not been determined. A Missouri state judge rejected this lawsuit.

Another question that remained unanswered was the identity of the mysterious Robert Odom. A Gore-Lieberman attorney, Douglas Dowd, said in an interview with KMOX radio, "Mr. Odom was introduced to me, for the first time I ever met him I asked him about whether he was registered, and so on, and he was ambivalent about it. Therefore, I informed him and the other people from the campaign that I could not, and would not, use him in the proceedings. I don't think anybody was trying to trick anybody."

The problems with Dowd's account are: a) he verified the petition listing Mr. Odom as a plaintiff as being truthful when it was handed in at 3:20 P.M.; b) he informed the court that Odom was present and prepared to testify; c) he never informed the court that he thought Odom was ambivalent about being registered; and d) Robert Odom was dead.

Kit Wager of the *Kansas City Star* was told by Democrats that the Odom mix-up might have been a typographical error and that the intended plaintiff was really "Robert M. Odom," also known as Mark Odom, a political operative for Bill Clay, the retiring congressman. But there is one problem with this explanation: Records show that "Mark Odom" voted between 2:00 and 3:00 P.M. that day, before the petition was filed. The information presented about Odom to Judge Baker before she issued her order was clearly false on its face.

In an interview with *Insight* magazine, Dowd changed his story again. "It really was a misunderstanding," Dowd insisted. "He [Mark Odom] thought he was going to be testifying that he saw all the chaos at the polls, but I thought he was one of the voters who had been turned down."

Dowd says he found out during the hearing that Odom had already voted, so he didn't have him testify. But Dowd never told Judge Baker or the appeals court that the named plaintiff, Robert D. Odom, did not exist, or that Mark Odom had in fact voted. He asserted, "There was no, in my judgment, legal or moral or ethical duty for me to say, 'Judge, Mr. Odom has voted.'"

Downtown

Douglas Dowd may have been a bit obtuse in his discussion of his mystery client, but he was correct in saying that hundreds of people were denied the right to vote on Election Day. St. Louis election officials kept an "inactive voters list" of people who hadn't voted in at least four years and had not returned cards verifying their addresses. Voters on the list, which ballooned to more than 54,000 names in a city where only 125,230 people voted, had a legal right to cast their ballots, but election officials had to confirm their registration with the election board downtown. Phone lines there were busy all day, and many people were told they should travel downtown to prove their eligibility before an election judge. After the election, the board settled a lawsuit by promising to have a copy of the inactive voters list available at every voting precinct and to upgrade its phone service.

But not everyone who went downtown was an eligible voter. There appeared to be an effort to flood the election board with voters regardless of whether they were registered; at many precincts, buses provided by the Democratic Party waited to ferry voters downtown. The election judges, all of them Democrats, issued close to five hundred orders allowing people to vote and never let Republicans challenge any of them.

Some of the orders were clearly rubberstamped. Judge Michael Calvin let Jean Y. Nelson vote even though the only justification for it was her written statement: "I am late registering due to me were [*sic*] going through a mental disorder." A Mary Ellis sought and was granted an order when her only reason was: "I Mary Ellis, was a [illegible] felon. I was released on November of 1999. I didn't know that I had to register again to vote." Domon Price was given an order without making any written statement. Judge Janalyn Oberkramber requested a ballot with the explanation: "Missed registration deadline date."

An attorney who was doing business in the St. Louis court building submitted an affidavit to the U.S. attorney in which he said he was in Judge Calvin's court on Election Day and looked "through a number of these petitions" from voters appearing before him and "between 75 percent and 85 percent of them had in the handwriting of the petitioner reasons which were invalid so far as being allowed to vote." When the judge addressed each petitioner, "there was no inquiry by the judge as to whether they had ever registered, attempted to register or anything of the kind." Later on Election Day, Judge Calvin and other judges moved to the lobby of the elections board, from which they issued more orders to the people waiting in line.

Missouri's secretary of state, Matt Blunt, later found that only 35 of the 1,268 court orders to vote met the legal standard set by Missouri law. Among the other excuses given by voters and accepted by election judges were: "I want a Dem. president"; "For the democratic party"; "I'm a busy lady w/ 7 children"; and "Found out about Gore from my mother."

The opera bouffe that transpired downtown surprised few court watchers in St. Louis, who know judges there are notorious for having a flexible attitude toward election laws. James Williams, a cook at Micky's Bar downtown, filed an affidavit stating that on the day before the 2000 election he noticed Judge Baker having lunch. She approached him on her way out to discuss the election. Mr. Williams told her that because he was now a St. Louis County resident, he couldn't vote in the city of St. Louis. She informed him that if he came to her chambers the next morning she would issue an order allowing him to vote in the city anyway. Several other employees of the bar joined the conversation at that point and told her they couldn't vote because they were convicted felons. She told them they could still vote if they had an order from her allowing them to do so and suggested they also come to her chambers for such an order. Her rationalization was that if they had been registered voters before their conviction, they should be able to vote.

Secretary Blunt's investigation of the 2000 election also detailed how the federal Motor Voter Law was facilitating fraud. He calculated that a total of 247,135 St. Louis residents, dead or alive, were registered to vote, as compared with the city's voting-age population of 258,532. That translated to a whopping 96 percent registration rate, the envy even of places like Pyongyang, where not voting is a capital offense. The secretary of state also made the following findings:

> Sixty-two (62) federal felons voted in that election along with fifty-two (52) state felons; Sixty-eight (68) people voted twice; Fourteen (14) dead people cast votes; Seventy-nine (79) people registered to vacant lots in the city of St. Louis voted in the election; 45 of the city's election judges were not registered to vote, as they are required to do in order to lawfully hold the position of election judge. 250 addresses [were discovered] that are not identified as apartments from which eight or more individuals are registered to vote. A random sampling of 54 of these locations indicates that 14 might have been used as drop-sites for multiple false voter registrations.

Democrats responded to the report by insisting that their only interest had been to ensure that as many people voted as possible. "I think we need to be leery that in the zeal of some of the individuals who are trying to keep rehashing Election Day that their ultimate goal isn't to stymie turnout in the city of St. Louis," said Jim Grebing, spokesman for the state

Democratic Party, when confronted with evidence of fraud. William Lacy Clay, by then the city's congressman, said he supported efforts to clean up the city's election record but he recommended that prosecutors recognize that if they targeted too many African Americans for investigation, their actions would be perceived as discrimination: "I'm concerned that this [investigation] will aggravate racial relations in this city," he warned darkly. Reverend Earl Nance Jr., a local minister, observed, "People in this community, white and black, read race into everything."

The Strange Case of Ritzy Mekler

The specter of election fraud quickly returned to St. Louis in early 2001, just in time for the mayoral primary. The difference was that this time all the major candidates were both Democratic and black. On the very last day to register to vote in the primary, someone dropped off 3,800 voter registration cards. Most were for alleged voters on two specific streets, most were written with identical handwriting, and most were fraudulent.

The brazenness of the fraud was stunning. One of the fraudulent registration cards belonged to Alberto "Red" Villa, a city alderman who had died ten years earlier. "Our election system in St. Louis is like Fort Knox without locks on it," said James Shrewsbury, an alderman whose deceased mother's name was found in the pile of new registrations.

Without a white/black dimension to inject emotional paralysis into the issue, action was swift. As a grand jury was convened, even the liberal *St. Louis Post-Dispatch* editorialized that the city "appears to have a full-blown election scandal," and that in any investigation, Governor Bob Holden must "show he can escape the pull of the Democratic machine" that delivered his narrow victory the previous November. (Governor

Holden eventually replaced all four members of the city's election board.)

Senator Kit Bond also won national attention for his complaints about the St. Louis scandal, which he called "a blot on the process at least as bad as anything that happened in Florida." In March 2002 he focused television network news coverage on the issue of vote fraud when he brought photos of Ritzy Mekler, a thirteen-year-old springer spaniel that had been registered to vote in St. Louis for eight years, to the Senate floor. Ritzy's owner, Margaret Mekler, suspects that her dog became a registered voter because she and her husband put their phone number under Ritzy's name to avoid having their own names in the phone book. "We got a voting identification card that said she had moved here from California, she was twenty-one and had a Social Security number," Mekler laughed. "My dog is very intelligent but I'm not sure I want her voting on who's going to be the president."

Senator Bond said that Ritzy's registration was no laughing matter. "I have a feeling that whoever wrote Ritzy Mekler on the registration form probably could duplicate that signature each and every time they wanted to vote," he told his Senate colleagues. Senator Chuck Schumer, a New York Democrat, responded dismissively by saying that no law Congress could pass would prevent all dogs from voting.

But Senator Bond's campaign led to an effort to do something about the situation that had led to absurdity and illegality in St. Louis. The new federal Help America Vote Act, which finally passed in 2002, included requirements that states set up statewide voter registration systems and ask photo identification of the small number of first-time voters who have registered by mail. That just might prevent someone from signing up Ritzy's relatives in the future.

Back in St. Louis, prosecutors finally swung into action after the 2001 primary registration confirmed that someone was padding the voter rolls with ghosts and had turned the city into a national laughingstock. Circuit attorney Jennifer Joyce made clear that the days when vote fraud would be merely winked at were over. "I want to send a message that our election system should not be tampered with," she told the *St. Louis Post-Dispatch.* "We invite such acts when we don't hold people accountable."

After a two-and-a-half-year investigation, Joyce finally brought indictments in November 2003 against nine people who worked for Operation Big Vote, a well-known registration program. But other than Nona Montgomery, the local manager of the program, the others were small-fry: temporary, hourly workers hired to register people on street corners and in shopping malls. Three bigger fish who testified before the grand jury in the case escaped indictment altogether. They included Darlene Green, the city comptroller; Pearlie Evans, a former district director for now-retired representative Bill Clay; and Keena Carter, the Democratic deputy director of the St. Louis Board of Elections.

Carter escaped Joyce's net because it turned out that board members are allowed to engage in partisan activities at the same time as they administer elections. In her political capacity, Carter attended a meeting with Nona Montgomery, the key figure in the fraud, on February 12, 2001. Both Green and Evans were also present. At that meeting, investigators say, a plan was hatched to destroy copies of the false registration cards in order to prevent them from being traced.

Carter agreed to testify on what happened during the meeting, and in exchange received immunity from prosecution. A month after the indictments, she was quietly taken off the paid administrative leave that the elections board had placed her on and reinstated to her duties overseeing St. Louis elections. "We discovered no wrongdoing," explained the board's new chairman, Derio Gambaro.

2002 Replay

The 2002 elections involved more close races in Missouri. The Republican candidate for U.S. Senate against Senator Jean Carnahan, the widow of the late governor Mel Carnahan, was Jim Talent, a former congressman and the losing GOP candidate for governor against Bob Holden in 2000. Intent on making sure this election was better policed than the last one, he deployed dozens of lawyers and poll watchers in St. Louis to monitor the voting. His point man was Thor Hearne, who had helped conduct an investigation of the 2000 St. Louis vote fiasco.

On election night, Hearne and Jack Bartling, a top aide to Senator Bond, were at Talent headquarters in St. Louis County. All the returns had come in by 10:30 P.M. except those from the city of St. Louis. Talent was narrowly ahead but Hearne was nervous because of the heavy Democratic vote that traditionally came out of St. Louis. He called Catherine Barondo, a counsel in the secretary of state's office who was at the election board office, to find out what the delay was about. She informed him that the board had run the punch-card ballots through the counting machines once and gotten a figure. But workers had just found some six hundred absentee ballots under the desk of an employee and now had to count those. They would also have to recount the votes they had already counted so that the new votes could be allocated to the proper precinct. The board wouldn't release any totals from the votes already counted until every vote had been tabulated.

Hearne and Bartling became suspicious, jumped into a car and barreled down the freeway toward downtown. Within fifteen minutes they were at the election board office. "I told them it was fine to count the new votes, it was fine to recount the old votes, but they had to give me a preliminary total," Hearne recalls. "The entire state had been counted except for

St. Louis and everyone knew how many votes Carnahan had to make up if she was going to win." Fearing a last-minute surge of mystery votes that would push her over the top, he asked for a total-in-progress. He was refused.

"A Democratic lawyer named Shauna Clements was there insisting that no totals could be released," he says. "She seemed to be intimidating the election officials who were standing around largely mute." For about ninety minutes, Hearne and Bartling demanded a preliminary total. Finally Rufus Tate, the election board's attorney, stepped forward and agreed to release a tally that excluded only the uncounted absentee votes. "That margin wasn't enough to overcome Talent's lead outside of the city," Mr. Hearne recalls. "Those absentee votes couldn't at that point have made the difference with the other votes publicly reported." Talent ended up winning the Senate seat by 21,000 votes.

Elections in St. Louis were a little less chaotic in 2002 than they were in 2000, but there was reason to worry again as presidential elections approached. In May 2004, the state auditor, Claire McCaskill (a Democrat), issued a scathing report on the election board's procedures in the primary held the previous month. It found that 24,000 of the city's voters, nearly 10 percent, were "questionable." The report tabulated 4,405 dead people, 2,242 felons, 1,453 people voting from vacant lots, and 15,963 also registered somewhere else in Missouri or Illinois. At least 935 of the felons, or some 40 percent, had apparently cast a ballot in a recent election.

McCaskill, now a U.S. senator from Missouri, concluded that the St. Louis Board of Elections was beyond repair. She said it needed "local control and direct accountability" and suggested that control of it be transferred directly to the mayor. Governor Bob Holden, a fellow Democrat, agreed.

In June 2004, another scandal broke when the Associated Press turned up evidence that America Coming Together, an anti-Bush group funded by $5 million from the financier George Soros, had hired dozens of felons to go door-to-door and register voters in Missouri, and also in Florida and Ohio, two other battleground states. ACT's counteroffensive was swift and predictable. First, the organization denied that it had employed violent felons. When the Associated Press reported that ACT employees did indeed include people convicted of assault and sex offenses, the group admitted it might have hired felons in fourteen other battleground states. It also promised to fire anyone guilty of "violent or other serious offenses." In some cases it won't have to; four felons it hired in Missouri have already been sent back to prison, one for endangering the welfare of a minor. That's one reason the Missouri Department of Corrections banned ACT from its list of potential employers for parolees in halfway houses. Noting that the felons would have to handle driver's license information and telephone numbers as part of the voter registration process, the department concluded that "from a public safety standpoint, we didn't want offenders to be in a situation where they would be handling that information."

ACT also denied that it was violating federal election laws that prohibited it from engaging in partisan activity on behalf of the Kerry campaign, even though its website said it was "laying the groundwork to defeat George W. Bush and elect Democrats." Its roster of staffers was chock full of Democratic operatives with close ties to Kerry. One ACT staffer, Rodney Shelton, left the organization to become the Kerry campaign's Arkansas state director, while the former Kerry campaign manager Jim Jordan joined ACT. Federal law forbids any coordination between a voter registration group like ACT and a political campaign, but the law is impossible to enforce.

ACT's president, Ellen Malcolm, said the attacks on her group represented an attempt "to distort and play politics with this situation, to attempt to disrupt ACT and our grassroots activities." But in light of the felon scandal, ACT's activities merit closer scrutiny because they may have made the problem of sloppy voter rolls worse. The Federal Election Commission has found that 12 percent of all registered voters nationally were "inactive voters" and thus subject to possible misuse by having someone else vote in their name.

St. Louis has improved its voter rolls in recent years, although the city had to endure yet another voter registration scandal in 2006—this one initiated by workers from ACORN, several of whom wound up being indicted. But Scott Linedecker, the co-chairman of the city's election board, says that all the conditions still exist for vote fraud to occur again in St. Louis. Just this year, he reports, evidence has turned up that some sixty dead people in the St. Louis area cast ballots in recent elections.

Twelve

Vote Fraud
the Old-Fashioned Way

WITH 40 PERCENT OF AMERICANS NOW BELIEVING that the election system is often subject to tampering, and with charges of fraud swirling around the 2004 as well as the 2000 presidential election, it's worth taking a look back at the nation's long tradition of electoral shenanigans. It's comic—until you start to wonder just how much of the same is still going on.

Nowhere did vote fraud have a more notorious record than in Tammany-era New York. Tammany Hall's ruthless efficiency in manufacturing votes—especially during the zenith of its power in the second half of the nineteenth century—is legendary. At the time, America didn't yet have privacy-protecting voting machines or official government ballots, so Tammany fixers could ensure that voters would cast ballots as promised. Vote riggers would simply give people premarked ballots and watch as they deposited them into the voting box.

Practical Tammany pols preferred to deal with "strikers"— wholesale operatives who would guarantee thick bundles of votes, for a price. One New York candidate who hadn't yet paid his strikers made the mistake of visiting the polls on Election Day. The angry operatives swiftly surrounded him, demanding their cash. Mark Summers, a historian, recounts that "the politician was nearly torn to pieces ... and as he fled the pack cursed him for 'a mean cuss' and emptied out the ballot-boxes, tearing up every ticket bearing his name."

The immigrants flooding into New York were easy prey for the Tammany pols. At the time, each state set its own standards for naturalizing new citizens, and New York's were lax. In 1868, *The Nation* reported that Tammany Hall had set up a "naturalization mill," instantly certifying folks right off the boat as citizens—and Tammany voters. (In 1996, the Clinton administration similarly sped up the naturalization of up to a million new citizens in time for them to vote in that year's election.)

Tammany was so efficient at election fixing that between 1868 and 1871 the votes cast in the city totaled 8 percent more than the entire voting population—"the dead filling in for the sick," as one contemporary wag put it. The historian Denis Tilden Lynch describes how thugs would go from one polling place to the next, impersonating citizens who hadn't yet voted.

One such "repeater" posed as the dignified pastor of a Dutch Reformed church. The election clerks asked him his name.

"Jones," shouted the repeater, startling the poll workers with his scraggly beard, unclean face and whiskey breath.

"What is the first name, Mr. Jones?" asked the election clerk.

"John," snarled the repeater.

"The Reverend Dr. John Jones, pastor of the Dutch Reformed church around the corner?" asked a clerk.

"Yes, you dirty, lousy @$#%%^**!" exclaimed the repeater. "Who'n else did you think I was, eh?"

The officials let "Reverend Jones" vote.

After his fall from power, the infamous Tammany Hall leader William Marcy Tweed—a.k.a. Boss Tweed—candidly assessed the conduct of elections in his city. His testimony before the New York Board of Aldermen in 1877 remains fascinating for its matter-of-fact explication of how to corrupt democracy:

Q: "When you were in office, did the [Tweed] Ring control the elections in the city at that time?"

A: "They did sir. Absolutely."

Q: "Please tell me what the modus operandi of that was. How did you control the elections?"

A: "Well, each ward had a representative man, who would control matters in his own ward, and whom the various members of the general committee were to look up to for advice on how to control the elections."

Q: "What were they to do, in case you wanted a particular man elected over another?"

A: "Count the ballots in bulk, or without counting them announce the result in bulk, or change from one to the other, as the case may have been."

Q: "Then these elections really were no elections at all? The ballots were made to bring about any result that you determined upon beforehand?"

A: "The ballots made no result; the counters made the result.... That was generally done to every ward by the gentleman who had charge of the ward."

Q: "Mr. Tweed, did you ever give any directions to any persons, to falsify or change the result of the actual bona fide ballots cast in any election?"

A: "More in the nature of a request than a directive."

Later in Tweed's testimony, this exchange occurred:

Q: "Can you state now, at this time, whether the election which took place in the City of New York at that time [1868] was a fair and honest election?"

A: "I have not the details in my memory."

Q: "What is your best impression?"

A: "I don't think there was ever a fair or honest election in the City of New York."

Tammany's fraud was so all-encompassing, says Mark Summers, that "even men who have passed through history with clean reputations thought little of raising a majority that way." Henry Raymond, co-founder and first editor of the *New York Times*, railed against corruption. But when he ran for speaker of the New York State Assembly in 1851, he asked Senator Hamilton Fish for $1,000 so that he could buy the election. "Truly a pretty suggestion," Fish confided to his diary, "but corruption in connection with these primary elections has become so prevalent that one loses astonishment at its evidence in any quarter."

Boss Tweed died in disgrace, but Tammany Hall flourished into the twentieth century. In 1905, William Randolph Hearst, owner of the *New York Morning Journal*, decided to take Tammany on and run for New York mayor on the ticket of his own third party, the Municipal Ownership League. Hearst had already beaten a Tammany-backed candidate in 1902, winning a New York congressional seat with a lavish campaign that would have put Senator Jon Corzine of New Jersey to shame. Hearst spent the equivalent of $100,000 for fireworks in Madison Square Park and offered free trips to Coney Island for every man, woman and child in his district.

But Hearst bit off more than he could buy in running for mayor—a key position in the Tammany empire. On Election Day, notes Hearst biographer David Nasaw, "there were instances of vote fraud, of poll watchers being chased away, of delays in reporting returns, of unopened and uncounted ballot boxes mysteriously turning up in the East River." The *New York Independent* declared it "the most extraordinary election ever witnessed in New York City"—and that's saying something. The *New York Times* reported that the challenger's poll watchers, having been beaten up and driven off by Tammany goons, "came into the Hearst headquarters last night with bandaged hands. Some carried their arms in slings. At about ten o'clock in the evening a report was received that the returns were being held back from these districts"—presumably as Tammany stuffed the ballot boxes to achieve the desired count. One poll watcher, R. Little, "had a finger chewed off and his face cut."

While the newspapers deplored the violence, they also expressed relief that the incumbent Tammany mayor George Brinton McClellan beat Hearst, by a margin of 3,472 votes out of more than 600,000 "cast." The *New York Times* congratulated city voters for having "spared the city the humiliation, the trials, and the dangers of a four years' mismanagement of its affairs by a peculiarly reckless, unschooled, and unsteady group of experimenters and adventurers."

Hearst believed that he had won the election as ballots went into the boxes but lost it as they came out. After organizing a blue-ribbon committee to protest the fraud and demand a recount, he held massive demonstrations throughout the city and went to court. But the courts and the state legislature ignored him, and no recount took place.

New York City's corruption, while severe, was far from unique. In Baltimore, for instance, vote fixing could get even uglier: a notorious Whig Party organization, the "Fourth Ward Club," hired thugs to seize innocent strangers and foreigners, drug them with bad whiskey and opiates, and send them out to cast multiple votes. (James Harrison, a biographer of Edgar Allan Poe, speculates that when Poe died in 1849 he was a victim of ruthless vote-fraud toughs who kidnapped him and left him drunk and near death on a Baltimore street.) Political scientists estimate that in many urban areas, fixers routinely manipulated 10 to 15 percent of the vote. A 1929 study by the Brookings Institution, looking back on U.S.

elections in the nineteenth century, observed that "indifference, fraud, corruption, and violence have marked the operation of our electoral system."

The corruption influenced national as well as local politics. Both major parties stole votes with abandon in the 1876 presidential election between Rutherford Hayes of Ohio and Samuel Tilden of New York. The race ended in a deadlock, resolved only after a congressionally created commission delivered the presidency to Hayes by a single, disputed electoral vote. At least three other presidential elections—in 1880, 1884, and 1888—proved so close that fraud may have played a role in their outcomes, too.

As the century closed, however, fraud gradually began to diminish, as popular disgust with vote rigging spurred reforms. States began to require voters to register before Election Day. In Massachusetts, Richard Henry Dana III, son of the author of the classic *Two Years Before the Mast*, persuaded the Massachusetts legislature to adopt the "Australian" ballot—a government-printed ballot that would list all candidates and that voters would cast in secret in a booth. It became a model for reformers elsewhere. As changes spread to other states, voter "turnout" fell precipitously. The historians Gary Cox and Morgan Krause point out that turnout in New York State elections dropped some 15 percent after the antifraud measures took effect.

Vote fraud didn't vanish from American politics, of course—jokes still circulate about the late Chicago mayor Richard Daley's uncanny ability to get the dead to vote for him. But first prize for twentieth-century electoral corruption goes to Mayor Frank "I Am the Law" Hague, whose political machine controlled gritty Jersey City, New Jersey, across the Hudson River from New York, from 1917 to 1947. His desk had a special drawer that opened in the front, allowing visitors to deposit bribes that then disappeared inside the desk. On a yearly salary of $8,000, he amassed a fortune of at least $10 million.

Hague's career began inauspiciously. Expelled from school after sixth grade as incorrigible, he became a ward heeler for the Jersey City Democratic machine. In 1908 he entered city employment as a janitor. Ten years later he was mayor and, through his control of the Hudson County vote, the leader of the state Democratic Party and the man who could dictate who would become governor or a judge. In 1939, so great was Hague's power that he could order his handpicked governor to appoint his son, Frank Hague Jr., to the state supreme court, even though the young man had never graduated from law school.

The Hague machine turned vote fraud into a science. On the Sunday before an election, the mayor would gather his ward heelers into a Jersey City arena (called the Grotto) and give his orders. "Three hundred and sixty-four days a year you come to me wanting favors.... Now, one day in the year I come to you." Hague fielded roughly one worker per 100 voters, and boy, did he get results. In 1937, the Democratic candidate in the First District of the First Ward won 433 votes, the Republican only one. This struck some people as odd, since a short time earlier the district had recorded 103 Republican votes. An investigation found torn ballots, others with unmistakable erasure marks, and yet others altered by pencil. The single Republican ballot, marked with a red pencil, "could not have been erased without doing definite damage to the ballot," investigators noted.

Reformers were always trying to clean up Jersey City elections, but they faced an uphill fight. In 1935, the Honest Ballot Association sent 245 Princeton students to monitor a city election. Hague's ruffians beat up five of them within an hour of their arrival. Several others, ejected from a polling place, went to the mayor to protest. "Well, you fellows go back there if you wish, but if you get knocked cold it will be your own hard luck," he told them. Later, Hague explained to *Collier's* magazine that the roughing-up involved "[a]nimal spirits, that's all. I told my boys to lay off, but it was a pretty dull election, and they couldn't resist the temptation to have a little fun."

In 1937, the *Jersey Journal* asked in a disgusted editorial: "Where was Election Superintendent Ferguson's 1,300 deputies when the new irregularities now charged occurred last Tuesday?" In response, the superintendent issued a public statement that read, in part: "Where were my deputies? Some of them were locked up in the police stations; some were stuck on corners, with a threat that if they moved from them, a night stick would be wrapped around their necks.... The only way to have an honest election in Hudson County under present conditions is with the militia."

Mayor Hague retired from office in 1947, turning over the job of mayor to his nephew. Gradually, his machine lost control of the city, though Jersey's politics remain far from pristine to this day. Nevertheless, Hague's flagrant vote rigging was extreme for post-Tammany American politics.

Yet if Hague's ghost, or Boss Tweed's, took a look at a recent newspaper, he'd smile in recognition. Wholesale vote fraud is on the rise again. In 2008, we should be well past the days of Boss Tweed.

Thirteen

The Ghost of LBJ

OST DEMOCRATS DOWNPLAY THE EXISTENCE OF
election fraud, but not Ciro Rodriguez, a former
chairman of the Congressional Hispanic Caucus.
He's from Texas, the capital of stolen elections. In March 2004
he lost his Democratic primary to Henry Cuellar, former
Texas secretary of state, in a redrawn district that stretches
from the barrios of San Antonio to the Mexican border at
Laredo.

Ciro Rodriguez initially led by 126 votes on election night,
but weeks later a recount of Cuellar strongholds in Webb
County (Laredo) and next-door Zapata County gave the challenger the lead. After another recount, Cuellar was ahead by
58 votes and certified the winner.

Rodriguez promptly challenged the result, claiming systemic vote fraud. Many observers agreed with him that South
Texas has a long history of incompetence and chicanery in voting. "There are still political bosses and questionable activities," says Geronimo Rodriguez, who was a regional director
for the Gore campaign in 2000. The recount in Zapata
County even turned up a missing ballot box with 304
uncounted votes, some 10 percent of the total cast in the
county. Over 80 percent of those votes went to Cuellar. Officials in Webb County reported that their recount came up
with 115 more votes than they had first reported. Cuellar won

every one of the newly discovered votes. A second recount of Webb County then mysteriously reduced Cuellar's vote there by 145 votes.

"It stinks to high heaven, to be honest with you," John Puder, a top adviser to Rodriguez, told me. But Doroteo Garza, the supervisor of the recount in Zapata, disputed any charges of chicanery. "The boxes were not tampered with— everything's there. The seals were not broken. The only thing we can suspect is that those ballots were there, but they were not counted." Nonetheless, some Rodriguez supporters saw the ghost of Lyndon Johnson striding again across the plains of South Texas.

Part of Texas political legend involves the way LBJ saved his career in 1948 when he was losing a Democratic primary for U.S. senator. A full week after the primary, an operative for George Parr, a political boss known as "the Duke of Duval County," adjusted the total of Ballot Box 13 in nearby Jim Wells County to include 200 additional votes for Johnson. That gave him an 87-vote victory statewide out of over a million cast. But the voters of Box 13 were an orderly bunch: they apparently had cast their ballots in exact alphabetical sequence. Nevertheless, Johnson's victory survived every legal challenge and set him off on a career path that eventually led to the White House.

J. K. Ray, an agent for the state's tax division, joined a Texas Ranger named Frank Hamer for an investigation of Box 13. When they arrived at a bank in Jim Wells County, the two men found it surrounded by armed *pistoleros*, thugs, and other assorted henchmen committed to an LBJ victory. Brandishing their guns, Hamer and Ray made their way through the crowd and into the building. They discovered men burning ballots and altering the voting rolls. Ray's granddaughter, Kay Daly Ryan, recalls: "He always said he witnessed the crux of the scam that permitted sheriff's deputies and election officials to steal the election for LBJ." In 1977, Johnson's biographer Robert Caro interviewed Luis Salas, the man in charge of Box 13, and after three decades of silence and denials got him to admit: "Johnson didn't win that day. We stole it for him."

Old-style ballot box stuffing isn't as easy in the Lone Star State today as it was back then, but there is still enough mischief for Texas to retain its status as a case study in election fraud. A cottage industry of get-out-the-vote organizers called *politiqueras*, or paid voter brokers, recruit the elderly and disabled to vote by mail. Dispensing advice, they sit nearby while voters mark their ballots in kitchens or living rooms. Often they will leave with the marked ballot, promising to stamp and mail it for the voter. "There is a lot of abuse. People complain to me that someone picked up their ballot, and they didn't even vote," says Guadalupe Martinez, chairman of the Jim Wells County Democratic Party. Jerry Polinard, a political scientist at the University of Texas, says of the *politiqueras*, "A person running for office ignores them at their peril."

Alfonso Casso, a former member of the Laredo City Council, says that the existence of "a one-party system where the literacy rate is low" perpetuates the practice of voters "selling their vote to the highest bidder without any regard or knowledge of the issues."

Herminia Becerra, an eighty-year-old grandmother who calls herself the queen of the *politiqueras* in Brownsville, says she is actually helping the average person, choosing candidates who will benefit the community. "We are the voice" of the community and "problem solvers," she claims. For the most part, criticism of her and her fellow *politiqueras* comes from an Anglo establishment that used to intimidate poor Hispanics, who only recently have gotten some political clout. This makes their criticism automatically suspect. Besides, adds Becerra, she backs candidates from both parties. In 2006, she even carried a campaign sign for Governor Rick Perry, a conservative Republican who nonetheless supported a guest worker agreement with Mexico.

But criticism of the vote brokers also comes from election officials. The Republican attorney general, Greg Abbott, has prosecuted twenty-six cases of vote fraud in the last couple of years. The most serious involved a former Port Lavaca City Council member who lied to a grand jury about registering noncitizens to vote and a Refugio County commissioner who gave mail-in ballots to residents to mark in his presence. Both were convicted and imprisoned. Others included a woman who voted for her dead mother and a man who voted twice.

Abbott has also had some reversals. This year a judge dismissed charges against three Hidalgo County women who were indicted on charges that they illegally assisted elderly voters in a 2005 mayoral race in McAllen. Hidalgo County's election administrator, Teresa Navarro, has nonetheless ended the practice of letting vote brokers pick up hundreds of applications for mail-in ballots after a large number of them were turned in with the same post office box listed as the home address.

Debra Danburg, a Houston Democrat who served as chairman of the election committee in the Texas House of Representatives until 2003, says the actions of many vote brokers are "victimizing the elderly.... I wish the older citizens' lobby group would see the fraud I'm seeing and start reacting like victims of fraud."

Republicans now have complete control of Texas state government but have been slow to implement reforms. "It's out of fear they will be tagged as racist and preventing elderly people from voting," says Congressman Ron Paul of Texas. But he says many Republicans are mistaken if they think fraud occurs only in Hispanic areas. "There's fraud in the suburbs. But it's done more subtly," he told me.

Ciro Rodriguez doesn't think much subtlety was involved in his 58-vote defeat. KENS-TV searched a partial list of two dozen suspect voters identified by the Rodriguez team in Webb County. Francisco Garcia of 12 Ventura Street in Laredo was listed as voting in person in the primary, but they couldn't locate his home. A few blocks over, Christina Vasquez of 319 Water Street was also listed as having voted, although homes on that side of the street were all swept away in a flood in 1998. Elder Murillo confirmed he had voted, but said none of the five other voters listed at his address had lived there for at least five years.

Rodriguez's attorney, John Ray, said that if the courts had granted his client a hearing, he would have presented evidence of several hundred suspect votes. But the Texas Fourth Court of Appeals rejected Rodriguez's request for a trial and his request for a new election.

T. J. Connolly, a Cuellar spokesman, says "we had recounts and an election certified." He notes that in any trial the Cuellar forces would have been able to present evidence of shenanigans in San Antonio, an area Rodriguez carried with 80 percent of the vote. Officials there caught a total of forty-two applications for mail-in ballots from dead people. Could others have slipped through?

We will never know exactly what voting irregularities took place in the race, and no one has linked Cuellar to anything improper. But the controversy certainly begs the question of why we are still wondering what goes on in Texas ballot boxes more than sixty years after Ballot Box 13 was discovered.

Gilberto Quezada, the author of a book on Texas' tainted history of vote fraud, says "There is a close correlation of events between what is happening now with Ciro and Henry and what happened in 1948." He says that he gave a copy of this book to Rodriguez before the 2004 primary. "I said, 'Ciro, be sure and read this.' I don't think he did."

This story, however, has a happy ending as far as Rodriguez's political career goes. In 2006, a federal court redrew the Texas congressional map again and put the former congressman in a new district with a Republican incumbent. Rodriguez ran in the district and won the seat in that year's Democratic landslide. Now he and Henry Cuellar have the awkward job of working with each other while they try to bury the hatchet over their bitter 2004 recount.

Fourteen

How to Steal an Election
from Jimmy Carter

IN SEPTEMBER 2005, THE TWENTY-ONE-MEMBER BIPARTISAN Commission on Federal Election Reform, headed by former president Jimmy Carter and former secretary of state James Baker, concluded five months of study on how to clean up our election systems. The eighty-seven recommendations, which included a call for voters to show photo ID at the polls and a cleanup of absentee ballot security issues, represent a gold-standard guide on how to restore public confidence in the running of elections. Slowly but surely, the changes are being implemented, but progress is still woefully incomplete.

Many of the changes suggested are no-brainers. Some, like requiring states to establish uniform procedures for counting provisional ballots, can help ward off legal challenges based on ballots being treated differently depending on where they were cast. Others, like putting states instead of local jurisdictions in charge of voter registration, may not be absolutely necessary but would probably lead to the development of more accurate lists more quickly.

A separate recommendation for "nonpartisan" administration of elections is aimed at preventing a repeat of Florida in 2000 and Ohio in 2004, where the secretaries of state had prominent roles in the presidential campaigns. As good-governance reform, it's useful not to have state election officials lending their names to national campaigns. Where possible, the appearance of conflict of interest should be avoided. At the same time, it's inevitable that the process for choosing an election administrator will involve politics of some kind. I think it's better to have a transparent system where both parties can watch each other closely and keep raw partisan finagling to a minimum—but those who push for a nonpartisan approach make some good points.

While some argument over the commission's recommendations was expected, nothing matched the outrage that was heard when it was learned that eighteen of the twenty-one commissioners concluded that voters should be required to present photo identification at the polls. The recommendation was tagged "controversial," even though opinion polls consistently show that well over 80 percent of voters favor the idea. If photo ID requirements are a controversy, how does one define a consensus?

The ID recommendation was particularly noteworthy, because while the commission concluded there was no evidence of "extensive fraud" in U.S. elections or cases of multiple voting, it found that "both occur, and could affect the outcome of a close election. The electoral system cannot inspire public confidence if no safeguards exist to deter or detect fraud or to confirm the identity of voters."

Susan Molinari, a former Republican congresswoman from New York who served on the commission, noted bluntly that, "In 2004, elections in Washington state and Wisconsin were decided by illegal votes." She continued, "In other states, notably the states of Ohio and New York, voter rolls are filled with fictional voters like Elmer Fudd and Mary Poppins."

Just three of the twenty-one commissioners dissented over the photo ID recommendation, and one was Tom Daschle (Democrat), former Senate majority leader. He likened the ID requirements to a "poll tax." But that racially charged analogy is bunk because the panel recommended that identification cards be provided at no cost to those who need them. And photo ID if anything makes it significantly less likely that someone would be wrongly turned away at the polls due to out-of-date registration lists or for more insidious reasons. In any case, the tacit acknowledgment by Carter and most of the other liberals on the commission that the integrity of the ballot is every bit as important as access to the ballot is a welcome one.

Critics of the ID recommendation are correct that it won't eliminate the problem. Much of the vote fraud taking place today occurs not at polling places but through absentee ballots. In some states, for example, party officials are allowed to pick up absentee ballots, deliver them to voters and return them, leaving opportunity for all manner of illegal behavior. Other states allow organizations to pay "bounties" for each absentee ballot they deliver, which provides an economic incentive for fraud. The commission recommended that states eliminate both practices. President Carter made clear that with an active outreach effort to find people who are not registered and give them ID, a national voter identification program "will help minority voting instead of deterring it." In response to critics, Carter called the ID proposal a "move forward in getting more people to vote. It would not restrict people from voting. It will be uniformly applied throughout the country, and it will be nondiscriminatory."

The Old South vs. Jimmy Carter

Many people were surprised at the intensity of Carter's support for measures to ensure election integrity. They need not have been. Few people know it, but his own political career was almost ended before it began when he was the victim of massive vote fraud in his first race for public office—for state senator in Georgia in 1962. Carter told the story of how he almost had his first race stolen from him in his 1992 book, *Turning Point.* James Fallows of *The Atlantic* called it "the best thing" Carter has ever written.

In 1962, Carter was a thirty-eight-year-old Naval Academy graduate who had returned home to Plains to run his family's peanut business. In the spring of that year, the Supreme Court turned politics in Georgia and other states upside down when it ruled in its famous *Baker v. Carr* case that legislative districts had to be roughly equal in population, according to the "one man, one vote" principle.

That decision meant dramatic change in Georgia, where local political bosses in rural areas had long exercised inordinate power because of a rule requiring that every county, no matter how small, had to have at least one seat in the legislature. Urban counties were thus shortchanged in terms of influence, while rural political bosses could lord it over a few thousand easily manipulated white voters. Blacks, of course, were almost never allowed to vote. Carter recalls that when a black man tried to register in Plains in 1962 he was chased away by a gun-wielding registrar.

In Carter's case, the Supreme Court decision meant that his county of Sumter was joined with the neighboring county of Quitman in a new state senate district. But Quitman was the effective property of Joe Hurst, a local boss who demanded absolute obedience to his orders. He wielded real power, because half of the three thousand people in the county received some form of welfare and he made a point of personally delivering the checks and establishing a connection between his political survival and the economic survival of his voters.

The Democratic primary for the state senate seat pitted Jimmy Carter against Homer Moore, Hurst's handpicked candidate. But Election Day showed how difficult Carter's challenge would be. There was a tradition in some Georgia counties that called for local officials to withhold the results until they saw which way the election was going. Then, mysteriously, enough votes were found to shift the vote to another candidate. Lyndon Johnson was the beneficiary of just such a tactic in 1948, when Ballot Box 13 was discovered days after the polls closed with just enough votes in it to give him a U.S. Senate seat by a margin of 87.

But Hurst didn't stop at a slow count to make sure Carter would lose. The graveyards were scoured for names of people who could return from the dead for just one day to help the boss out a final time. Hurst also moved the polling station in Quitman's biggest town, Georgetown, from a spacious public building to a cramped office where he could force voters to mark their preference in full view of himself or his stooges.

Sometimes even that didn't suffice for Hurst's purposes. According to a Carter campaign worker, Hurst challenged an elderly couple after they had voted: "Wait a minute, Mr. Spear, and let me see if you all have learned the right way to vote. You know I have been trying to teach you for a long time."

After noting that the couple had voted for Carter, Hurst lost his temper. According to the campaign worker, he tore up the two ballots and said: "Give me some fresh ballots and let me teach them one more time." He then took six ballots and openly scratched out Jimmy Carter's name on all six, folded them and deposited them in the ballot box. "That's the way you are supposed to vote," he told the couple. "If I ever catch you all voting wrong again, your house might burn down!"

Carter's legal team collected a great deal of evidence of fraud and sought to overturn his 139-vote loss in the primary. They compiled files showing that votes had been cast for people who were out of town, in prison, and falsely registered. In addition, some precincts showed voters casting ballots in alphabetical order. Despite all this, Hurst had the election review committee in Quitman summarily dismiss Carter's complaint without a hearing. But Carter persisted and won a hearing before a state judge, Carl Crow.

In court, it became clear that something was wrong. A ballot box from Quitman was brought in and its seals were found to be faked, the stubs for all the ballots had been "lost," and a total of 431 votes had been cast even though only 333 people had shown up to vote. Hurst allies said the excess votes represented absentee ballots, which couldn't be produced because they were "missing." Judge Crow ruled that Carter had indeed won the election and was able to order that Carter's name appear on the general election ballot with just hours to spare. The power of the Quitman machine was broken. Joe Hurst ended up in jail on a moonshine charge, which is akin to Al Capone going to prison for income tax evasion.

But problems persisted in Georgia for years afterward. Carter recalls a 1964 debate in the state senate in which another state senator moved a tongue-in-cheek bill that declared, "No person may vote either in the Democratic primary or in the general election in the State of Georgia who has been deceased more than three years." Carter writes, "There followed a lively debate concerning the exact time interval between death and the loss of voting privileges."

The political experience of seeing his first election almost stolen from him made Carter a lifelong proponent of election reform. After his presidency he founded the Carter Center, which advises countries all over the world on best election practices and monitors results for fairness and accuracy. But the work of the Carter-Baker Commission may go down as his most lasting contribution to ensuring election integrity.

Conclusion

Where Do We Go from Here?

MARSHA TEMPLE IS A LAWYER FOR THE HEALTH-CARE group "End-of-Life Choices" in Los Angeles. Her husband, Warren Olney, hosts his own talk show on National Public Radio. Both are sophisticated observers of the political scene and active in civic affairs in Southern California.

A few years ago, Marsha decided she wanted to help out the Los Angeles County registrar's office during the upcoming primary; so she volunteered to work up to four hours that day. She got a perfunctory thanks, but otherwise never heard back from the registrar until the Friday before the election, when a truck pulled up to her home near Venice Beach and unloaded several boxes containing voting machines and all the equipment needed to run a precinct.

"What is this?" Marsha asked the driver.

"It's your polling place," he replied. "You're going to be manning one all day next Tuesday in the recreation room of a nearby school."

Floored, Temple tried to call the registrar but got only a busy signal.

Knowing how short the election authorities were on volunteers—especially those under age sixty-five with sufficient stamina—Marsha resigned herself to being in charge for a fourteen-hour day rather than helping someone else for four hours, as she had planned. On election morning she and her husband drove down to the school, unloaded seven voting machines and set up shop as a polling place. Everything went smoothly, with voters drifting in and out during the day in a low turnout. At no time had Marsha heard from anyone in the registrar's office. Sometime around noon, someone from the secretary of state's office came around, poked his head inside, asked if everything was all right, and then left. That was it as far as their contact with the government that day.

At the end of the day, Marsha and Warren packed up the machines, collected the ballots, and prepared to drive them to the registrar's office. "I stood there and suddenly realized how vulnerable our election process is," recalled Olney. "We had hundreds of blank ballots, a signature book of voters where we could have added more names. We made a list of how we could have easily added votes that didn't exist to the totals and no one would have been the wiser. The county barely knew who we were. We realized how much we have an honor system of voting and counting in this country."

An aide in the registrar's office I spoke with admitted that Olney had a point, but said that safeguards are in place that would have prevented him from pulling off a vote heist. But apparently those safeguards were secret, because she couldn't tell me what they were. And the issue of safeguards brings us to the part of any book where an author, having identified a problem, proposes some remedies. In the previous chapters, we've seen the chaos and larceny that menace our election process. How do we restore and preserve its integrity, especially at a time when so many people have become so disenchanted with it?

The leaders in any society are unlikely to change their habits or the rules they lay down for others unless pressured to do so by the governed. If corruption exists, it is in part because we the people permit it, either by silence, by inattention or by misunderstanding. If persistent vote fraud and outdated election procedures are to be remedied, the public and the media will have to demand it. Ignoring or refusing to recognize the enduring problems of election fraud and mismanagement that plague many parts of our country will ensure that it spreads, mutates, and grows more toxic.

"Easier to Vote, Harder to Steal"

When Congress passed the Help America Vote Act (HAVA) in 2002, its lead Democratic sponsor, Senator Chris Dodd of Connecticut, praised it for "making it easier to vote and harder to steal." But clearly HAVA is a first step. "Progress has been inadequate," said Robert Pastor, executive director of the Commission on Federal Election Reform, the panel cochaired by Jimmy Carter and James Baker in 2005 to address election issues left unresolved by HAVA.

HAVA's most important reforms require that states meet two "minimum standards" in conducting their elections. One mandates that states set up a centralized, statewide voter registration list to avoid duplications and limit how often a flawed voter list prevents someone from voting. By late 2004, only a dozen states will have completed the creation of these lists.

The other generally positive reform in HAVA is a requirement that every voter in every state be allowed to cast a "provisional" ballot if he or she shows up at a precinct and finds that his or her name is not on the registration list. For example, someone may have registered at a state Department of Motor Vehicles office while renewing a driver's license, but the DMV did not properly forward the registration application. If the authorities determine after the polls close that the voter was eligible, the vote counts. The way the system works now, provisional ballots are held until the polling place is closed on Election Day and then forwarded to the local election official or board of elections for a determination of whether the individual was really registered and eligible to vote. Once the election officials decide whether or not the provisional ballot should be counted, the voter can discover whether his vote was counted, and if not, the reasons why it was not counted at a toll-free telephone number or website.

HAVA also requires that any person who votes after the established time for polls to close due to a court order or other administrative decision to extend the polling hours must use a provisional ballot, and those provisional ballots have to be kept separate from all other provisional ballots. Otherwise, if there is a challenge to the extension of polling deadlines, the extra ballots have disappeared into the anonymity of the ballot box and cannot be "uncounted." This actually occurred in St. Louis in 2000 when lawyers for the Democratic Party were able to obtain an order that extended polling hours based on the claim that there were long lines at the polling places. But that ruling was later overturned as invalid because the named plaintiff in the suit had actually been dead since 1999. Thousands of extra votes were cast—and counted.

Provisional voting can be a real safety net for someone who is the victim of a bureaucratic mistake by a local election board, something that happens all too frequently. It also means that election judges spend less time during polling hours investigating why someone isn't listed on the rolls.

But provisional voting raises some serious concerns as well, since the ordinary safeguards against fraud do not apply. Normally, individuals must be on the voter registration lists in order to cast ballots. Allowing nonregistrants the ability to vote must be accompanied by safeguards to ensure that authorities count only legal votes. Because the federal rules on implementing provisional ballots are general, it has been left up to each state to issue detailed procedures on how to handle them. For that and other reasons, provisional ballots remain one of the most likely issues to spur lawsuits in the next election.

Indeed, thorny legal issues have already cropped up. In 2002, Congress mandated that a provisional ballot must be given to any individual whose name is not on the list of registered voters (or whose right to vote is challenged) if he "declares that such individual is a registered voter in the jurisdiction in which the individual desires to vote." But Congress's use of the word "jurisdiction" without defining it led quickly to lawsuits trying to overturn the tradition of precinct-based voting and allow voters to cast ballots anywhere in a state.

A blizzard of lawsuits were filed before the 2004 election in battleground states such as Florida, Missouri, Michigan and Ohio, in which the Democratic Party and other organizations including ACORN and the NAACP claimed that the word "jurisdiction" as used in the HAVA section on provisional ballots had a much wider meaning than the local precinct where an individual was assigned to vote based on residence. In essence, they claimed that Congress had preempted the tradition of precinct-based voting and that states were required to count the provisional ballots that were cast outside the voter's precinct. Thirty states and the District of Columbia require provisional ballots to be cast in the correct precinct to be counted, while fifteen states will count a provisional ballot cast in the correct jurisdiction, such as a municipality, county or state, but in an incorrect precinct.

The plaintiffs lost their cases in Florida and Missouri and won in Michigan and Ohio. The Florida and Missouri cases were not appealed, but the U.S. Court of Appeals for the Sixth Circuit overruled the Ohio decision. The court held that there was no evidence in the statute or the legislative history of HAVA that Congress intended to override the historic tradition of precinct-based voting in the United States.

Although HAVA required the states to provide a provisional ballot to an individual trying to vote outside his assigned precinct, states did not have to count that provisional ballot. This litigation leads one to speculate on whether the people filing it really believe that voters are so ill informed that they do not even know which precinct they live in and where they are supposed to vote—information that is contained on every voter's registration card and on sample ballots mailed before elections. One could, of course, speculate on a more sinister motive since the Sixth Circuit also pointed out that one of the main reasons behind traditional precinct-based voting is that "it makes it easier for election officials to monitor votes and prevent election fraud."

The upshot of mandating provisional voting in the 2004 election was that almost two million individuals cast a provisional ballot, about 2.56 percent of all the ballots cast in polling places on Election Day. At least 1.2 million of those ballots ended up being counted, or 64.5 percent. Washington State had the highest rate of provisional ballots at 11.3 percent of the votes cast at polling stations, followed by Alaska, 10.6 percent; Arizona, 9.0 percent; and California, 8.5 percent.

The U.S. Election Assistance Commission concluded in a report that there was no clear pattern of provisional ballots affecting the margin of victory in the 2004 presidential contest. However, in an interesting contrast between "red states" and "blue states," the jurisdictions in which President Bush won a plurality of the vote reported the lowest incidence of provisional ballots, representing just 0.5 percent of the ballots cast in polling places, while those jurisdictions that were won by John Kerry by more than 55 percent reported the highest incidence of provisional ballots, 3.28 percent of ballots cast in polling places.

The EAC also reported that the highest percentage of provisional ballots were cast in predominantly Hispanic jurisdictions (2.81 percent), followed by predominantly Native American jurisdictions (1.89 percent) and African American areas (1.28 percent). This may help explain the anxiety that the Democratic Party felt in 2004 in trying to force states to count provisional ballots cast outside the traditional polling place: the rules governing provisional ballots would seem to affect those voters who usually vote Democratic more than they do Republican voters.

All this is important because it means that provisional ballots could become the equivalent of Florida's chads and the infamous punch-card ballots in a future close presidential race. During the aftermath of the 2000 presidential election, both political parties and presidential campaigns sent thousands of volunteers and lawyers to Florida to observe the recounting of punch-card ballots and to argue and litigate over every ballot and whether it should count as a vote for their respective candidates. In 2000, only about one-third of the country besides Florida used punch-card ballots, but HAVA has ensured that 100 percent of the country must use provisional ballots.

A tug of war over provisional ballots may be inevitable in key states where the margin of victory is no greater than the number of provisional ballots cast. Both campaigns would once again send squadrons of lawyers to any closely contested state to watch and argue as every single provisional ballot in every election jurisdiction in the state is reviewed and a determination is made by local election officials as to whether it should be counted. Results could once again be delayed for weeks if not months after Election Day.

How likely is this to happen? In 2002, there was a thirty-five-day delay in determining the winner of Colorado's Seventh Congressional District when Republican Bob Beauprez led Democrat Mike Feeley by only 386 votes after the election. But there were 3,800 outstanding provisional ballots to be examined, and each of the three counties in the district had different rules on which ballots should be tossed out and which ones should be counted.

One county used a provisional ballot that didn't comply with the one provided by the Colorado Secretary of State's Office. Matters weren't helped by the fact that the secretary of state had to issue six different rule interpretations to the counties on how they should count the ballots. One memo sent on November 7 from Bill Compton, director of Colorado's elections division, created more panic than clarity among county election officials. It read:

> We need each of you to read between the lines on the memo regarding provisional ballots.... Please remember, SUBSTANTIAL COMPLIANCE is all that is necessary for the conduct of elections under Title One [of the Civil Rights Act]. Please use your common sense and best judgment in this process.

Such rule-shifting directives didn't help matters or inspire confidence in the overall count. The resulting chaos took weeks to resolve. In the end, Beauprez was declared the winner by 121 votes on December 10.

In the 2004 presidential election, there were 668,408 provisional ballots cast in California, a key electoral state. Florida, whose electorate decided the 2000 presidential election by fewer than a thousand votes, had 27,742 provisional ballots cast in 2004. Ohio, a key swing state, had 157,714 provisional ballots in the 2004 election. If the race between George Bush and John Kerry had been closer and Kerry had chosen to contest the results, the battles over provisional ballots in those states could have been monumental and delayed the outcome for months.

In 2008, it took the New Mexico Democratic Party almost ten days to determine the winner of its presidential primary because Senator Hillary Clinton's margin of victory was smaller than the number of provisional ballots that had been cast in the race. Out of a total of 149,779 votes cast in the primary, Clinton won by only 1,709 votes, receiving 4,215 provisional ballots to Barack Obama's 3,935. In this election, the campaigns and the Democratic Party had agreed ahead of time on what the rules would be for the counting of provisional ballots—but that is not likely to happen in a combative contest between two presidential campaigns of opposing parties.

Imagine the litigation—similar to the "equal protection" claims raised in the *Bush v. Gore* decision before the Supreme Court—over the different rules that states (or even different counties within states) apply to determine whether a provisional ballot is counted or not. Claims may be made over how much investigation a local election official must do to determine if an individual voter's registration paperwork was somehow lost or not forwarded to election officials by another government agency like the Department of Motor Vehicles or even a third-party organization such as ACORN that was conducting a voter registration drive. The fights and legal maneuvering over the counting of provisional ballots in a future election could make the chad fight in Florida in 2000 look like a mere dress rehearsal for a legal meltdown in several states at the same time.

It doesn't take a visionary to see that in the absence of clear rules, we can expect lawyers to try and turn the most implausible legal theory into a court ruling in their favor. Vague rules on provisional voting could create a nightmare in which the results of the presidential race aren't known for days. Recall the thirty-five days it took Colorado officials to decide one congressional race.

A Question of Identity

The most often discussed proposal to limit fraud and irregularities at the polls is a requirement that all voters show photo

ID before voting, much as they now do when they take an airline flight, donate blood, buy an Amtrak ticket, cash a check, rent a video or check into a hotel. Poll after poll shows the concept is popular and easily understood by the American people.

Yet this is one of the most bitterly fought reforms.

Opposition to photo ID laws has often reached comical levels. In the 1990s, the Clinton administration managed to come up with a public policy argument that people had to show a photo ID to buy cigarettes, while a state could not fight election fraud by requiring photo ID. The circus began in February 1997 when the Food and Drug Administration issued decrees against teen smoking, which ordered all stores that sell tobacco to demand photo ID from everyone who looks to be twenty-seven years or younger. At the same time, the Clinton Justice Department contended that Louisiana was out of bounds in asking adult voters to prove they really were who they said they were.

The Justice Department position was ironic given that Louisiana had just gone through a fresh election scandal. In the spring of 1997, the U.S. Senate was investigating allegations that the 1996 razor-thin election of Mary Landrieu, a Democrat, to a Senate seat was hopelessly tainted by thousands of phantom votes, including 1,380 people registered at abandoned buildings. A New Orleans assistant city attorney resigned in protest over irregularities in the Landrieu race, and Morris Reed, a judge and unsuccessful black candidate for city attorney, has charged election fraud in New Orleans.

State legislators in Louisiana had recognized that their state needed to clean up its act back in 1994, after the *Lake Charles American Press* decided to test the system by sending twenty-five fictitious applications signed only with an "X" to eight different voter registrars. Twenty-one were approved and put on the rolls, an 80 percent success rate in cheating.

Eye-popping examples such as this prompted Louisiana's legislature, led by state senator (later governor) Mike Foster, to require that voters who registered by mail show photo identification, though only when they voted for the first time.

But Louisiana was one of the states required by the Voting Rights Act to "preclear" changes in its election laws with the U.S. Justice Department. Justice threw out the ID provision on grounds that black voters are less likely to hold driver's licenses than white people. Justice also claimed that the Louisiana law imposed a more restrictive ID requirement on voters who register by mail. After much public ridicule over its contradictory stance regarding cigarette buyers, the Clinton administration finally dropped its objections to the Louisiana photo ID law, resolving the contradiction between the position of its Justice Department and the regulations issued by the FDA.

In the states that now also require *all* voters to present some form of documentation at the polls, ample provision is made for voters without a driver's license. Other acceptable forms of identification include the photo ID that driver's license bureaus issue to nondrivers, a utility bill, a paycheck, military ID or any other piece of information that might include a picture, date of birth, home address or signature. Those who lack the acceptable ID must in every state be allowed to sign an affidavit and cast a provisional ballot that is counted later, after the voter's eligibility is confirmed.

Many more states have considered a photo ID requirement for all voters since the 2000 Florida debacle. Legislatures in New Hampshire, Wisconsin, Iowa, Arizona and Kansas passed such laws only to see Democratic governors veto them.

In some states, the debate has been ugly. In Mississippi, a state with bad memories of civil rights workers being murdered for registering blacks, the debate over a photo ID bill was at first incendiary. David Jordan, a Democratic state senator from Greenwood, called the idea "rotten from the core. It is evil. It is wrong.... This is a back door to a poll tax." Another senator recalled the days when dogs in his Delta hometown were set loose on African Americans trying to vote. Bills to impose photo ID in the legislature have been stymied for years.

Then in district court in 2006, Judge Allen Pepper ordered the state legislature to enact the photo ID requirement. He handed down the ruling in response to a lawsuit by the Mississippi Democratic Party seeking to bar Republicans from voting in Democratic primaries. The judge granted the request, but in the process, he stipulated that all voters must reregister and present photo ID as the best way to ensure that the primaries could be closed to voters of another party.

This was not the solution that Democrats wanted, and they quickly appealed the ruling to the U.S. Court of Appeals for the Fifth Circuit. In May 2008, the court overturned Judge Pepper's order. "The state is divided.... We will put the parties out of their litigation misery," wrote Chief Judge Edith H. Jones, leaving Mississippi still divided over the issue and without a photo ID requirement.

Same-Day Registration

The other most talked about reform of the election system—which is not a reform at all but an added opportunity for mischief—comes from those who believe it is vitally important to make sure as many people as possible vote. Their favorite reform is same-day voter registration, which would allow new voters to register on Election Day. It is now used in Wisconsin, Minnesota and four smaller states.

In 2002, two liberal millionaires put the idea on state ballots in California and Colorado. They argued that registration deadlines of fifteen days before Election Day in California and thirty days in Colorado prevented some people from voting. Their proposals would have allowed anyone to show up at the polls, present a driver's license or some other document with his name and address on it, register on the spot and vote.

State and local election officials were generally opposed. Colorado's secretary of state, Donetta Davidson, said the program would prevent counties from checking for fraud and would require her to train thousands of poll workers to handle new computer equipment. In California, Connie McCormack, then the voter registrar of Los Angles County, warned that "Elections are in danger of collapsing under the weight of their own complexity." Other registrars opposed Proposition 52, as the same-day registration idea was identified, because it would not require "provisional ballots" for those who register on Election Day. (Current law requires that people whose eligibility is in dispute have their ballots kept separate and verified later.) If the initiative had passed, voters who registered on Election Day would have had their ballots mixed in with everyone else's. If investigators later proved there was fraud, there would be no way to know who was responsible. An aide to Bill Jones, California's secretary of state at the time, warned that under Proposition 52, busloads of people could "move into" a close, targeted district for a day and vote, then leave town, without technically breaking the law.

Mary Kiffmeyer, former Minnesota secretary of state, says she is tired of hearing her state's "same-day" registration extolled. She compares it to holding a party and not knowing how much food to buy because no one sent in an RSVP. Some precincts run out of ballots, while others are overstocked. "We have long lines because of same-day," she says. "People get frustrated and leave."

The states that have tried same-day registration are mostly small, with stable populations and long traditions of good government. Even so, problems crop up. In 1986, Oregon voters overwhelmingly scrapped the idea after a cult that wanted to take over a town government tried to register hundreds of supporters on Election Day. In 2000, a New York socialite working for Al Gore scandalized Wisconsin when a TV camera caught her bribing street vagrants with packs of cigarettes if they went to the polls. She pleaded guilty to fraud. At Marquette University in Milwaukee, 174 students boasted that they had voted more than once. They quickly changed their story when prosecutors pointed out that voting twice is a crime. Also that year, the U.S. Postal Service returned at least 3,500 Election Day registration confirmations as undeliverable in Wisconsin—meaning that thousands of people had registered to vote and probably cast ballots with the wrong address on Election Day. For what it's worth, Al Gore won Wisconsin by 5,700 votes.

Even some supporters of Election Day registration in smaller states quail when asked about its use in America's most populous state. Curtis Gans, director of the Committee for the Study of the American Electorate, says the risk of fraud in California is too great. "It's not beyond the imagination that one party or another will register aliens on the last day," he said. "And there's no protection against that except criminal penalties, which have not been effective."

Proponents of same-day voter registration spent millions in both California and Colorado promoting their initiative. But liberal newspapers shrank from the idea, with the *San Francisco Chronicle*, the *Los Angeles Times* and the *Denver Post* all editorializing against it. Even California's liberal governor Gray Davis opposed the idea. "His view is that voters who go to the polls ought to have a minimum amount of information about what they are voting on," explained Davis aide Garry South. On Election Day, same-day registration lost 59 to 41 percent in California, trailing in 45 out of 53 congressional districts. In Colorado, it won less than 40 percent of the vote, losing even liberal strongholds such as Denver and Boulder.

Same-day registration is the latest gimmick dreamed up by people who say they want to boost voter turnout. We've been down this road before. Motor Voter laws allow people to register to vote at the Department of Motor Vehicles. Liberal absentee voter laws let people cast ballots while on vacation or from remote locations. And some states allow for early voting, before Election Day. All these provisions have failed to increase voter turnout. It's about time that someone stepped forward and admitted that the root cause of low turnout isn't restrictive voting laws, but voter apathy. People are fed up with mediocre candidates, gerrymandered districts and uncompetitive (and possibly illegitimate) elections.

Rein in Voter-Chasing Lawyers

If we don't invest in better election procedures and equipment as well as voter education, we may pay for our failure by turning Election Day into Election Month through a new legal quagmire: election by litigation. "After Florida in 2000, election night is not necessarily the finish line anymore," says Doug Chapin, who runs Electionline.org, a clearinghouse of voting information. "Both sides are lawyering up to hit the ground running if anything happens."

Something is guaranteed to happen. You can bet that in a country of 170,000 polling places, some screw-ups and chicanery are inevitable. Some 20 percent of Americans will be using controversial new electronic voting machines that will become a magnet for lawsuits. But over 55 percent of Americans will use paper ballots, which while simple to use are easily manipulated. "Since 2000, upwards of 70 to 75 percent of the nation has changed voting equipment," Kim Brace, president of Election Data Services, told the *Boston Globe*. "Every time you make a change, it has the potential of causing problems.... Inevitably, the biggest problems occur the first time you use new equipment."

For their part, Republicans are conducting training sessions to respond to complaints of absentee ballot fraud, duplicate registrations and elderly residents of nursing homes being overly "assisted" in marking their ballot. They promise to have lawyers monitoring as many as 30,000 precincts or about one-seventh of the country. GOP lawyers also fear that in a close election, Democratic lawyers will take advantage of a flood of provisional ballots cast by people who aren't on the voter rolls and demand that all of them be counted regardless of eligibility, reprising the "Count Every Vote!" chant from Florida.

Democrats, who scoff that GOP concerns about election fraud are a cover for attempts to intimidate voters, are certain to outgun the Republicans in the legal arms race. One reason is that the overwhelming support of trial lawyers for Democrats. For example, Fred Baron, a former president of the Association of Trial Lawyers of America, was a top fundraiser for John Edwards in both 2004 and 2008. In 2002, ATLA became the largest single contributor to federal candidates, almost exclusively to Democrats. They are an even more important ally of the Democratic Party today. The 2000 Florida recount also allowed trial lawyers to make the argument to Democrats that lawyers could be as important as voters in determining elections and they should invest heavily in legal muscle. The trial lawyers have an enormous stake in Democratic victories in 2008.

In 2002, trial lawyers were extremely active in Democratic efforts to prepare for post-election litigation. Lance Block, former president of the Academy of Florida Trial Lawyers, boasted that his office was "ground zero" for the deployment of Democratic lawyers to polling places. In Colorado, a Democratic request to the Colorado Trial Lawyers Association for pro bono election help was swiftly forwarded to all its members. In 2004, trial lawyers even showed up at some precincts with signs around their necks, so voters with a problem could turn to a voter-chasing lawyer on the spot.

Who will monitor the lawyers as they turn American politics into another breeding ground for endless litigation?

Vanishing Volunteers

America has a vanishing corps of Election Day poll workers, as elderly workers retire or die and it becomes increasingly difficult to convince younger generations to take on a job that involves fourteen-hour days without a break and pays between $65 and $120 for the whole day. The complexity of election laws has made the job increasingly stressful and added the possibility of verbal or other abuse from angry voters. There is also the possibility of election workers being sent on wild-goose chases. Carol Anne Coryell, the former nonpartisan election administrator of Fairfax County, Virginia, recalls that during the 2000 presidential election she was constantly getting complaints from Democratic lawyers about voters being disenfranchised. "It got to the point where I would almost call it harassment," she says. "I checked with both the Democratic and Republican election official at every precinct where there were reports of people not being able to vote, denied the right to vote, and even people having to recite their Social Security number in public. None, I mean none, checked out. They took me away from real problems I should have dealt with."

"The lack of poll workers is a huge problem across the nation, and it's only going to get worse if states and counties don't act quickly," says Kay Albowicz of the National Association of Secretaries of State. "When the current crop gets to where they can't stand the long days, there's probably not going to be very many people to replace them."

The shortage of poll workers is already affecting the integrity of some elections. In March 2002, an unprecedented number of polling-place workers didn't report for work in Los Angeles County. A total of 124 precincts opened late and one didn't open at all. Now the county registrar, Connie McCormack, increasingly has to use county workers who get their regular pay for eight hours, but no overtime. She and other election officials know that's not a long-term solution.

Most of the election officials I interviewed estimated that the average age of their poll workers was in the late sixties. But with the increasing importance of technology in the election process, there is a greater need than ever for the technical talents of young people.

Some efforts are under way that would turn college students and graduating seniors in high school into poll workers. The Help America Vote Foundation is working with states to change laws that require poll workers to be over eighteen and registered voters. Their hope is that young people who work at the polls as an understudy to an older poll worker may become engaged enough to want to help out after they leave school.

Students who aren't up to being full-fledged poll workers could also help. The technologically savvy can explain the voting machines to those who need an explanation. They can help new and elderly voters understand the process. They can assist disabled voters who need help to get to the polling place. Some can even serve as translators.

Compounding the challenge of involving young people in the election process is the fact that in many schools, civics is no longer part of the curriculum. In his Farewell Address as he left the presidency in 1989, Ronald Reagan warned of the consequences of not educating Americans in their history. "If we forget what we did, we won't know who we are," he said. "I am warning of an eradication of the American memory that could result, ultimately, in an erosion of the American spirit. Let's start with some basics: more attention to American history and a greater emphasis on civic ritual."

Few would argue that since 1989 we have paid enough attention to Reagan's warning. We may be paying part of the price for that neglect every election cycle, when it becomes harder and harder to find enough poll workers. A shorthanded election process will eventually become a process that shortchanges the people.

Absent Rules, Enter Fraud

Absentee ballots represent the biggest source of potential election fraud because of the way they are obtained and voted. "All of us know that absentee voting is our least well protected part of the election process," says Doug Lewis, executive director of the Election Center, a Houston-based clearinghouse for the National Association of State Election Directors. A few simple steps would make it more difficult to abuse absentee ballots.

The envelope that an absentee ballot is placed in should be signed by the voter in the presence of at least one witness whose address and phone number are provided. Only the voter should be allowed to request an absentee ballot, not the voter's family members, because a request by a third party makes it impossible to compare the signature on a request form with the voter's signature file. Third parties such as campaign workers should be barred from delivering absentee ballots. This would prevent the alteration of ballots by campaign organizations and others.

States should be required to run computer comparisons on a regular basis to match their voter lists with death records and corrections department files so as to delete deceased individuals and felons who are ineligible to vote. Currently, the proce-dures in most states are inadequate and slow.

Federal immigration officials should also change their administrative procedures to allow immigration data to be used by local election officials to better police the voter regis-tration rolls. During a bitter recount of an Orange County congressional race, California's secretary of state found that in just one five-month period a minimum of 125 registered vot-ers had declined to serve on juries because they were nonciti-zens. Cases were turned over to local prosecutors, but no charges were filed.

State election officials should be authorized to establish a national central death registry that would collect information on all deaths from state vital records agencies and provide each state with the information needed to purge deceased vot-ers. Even states that have good record-keeping systems do not receive data on registered voters who have died outside the state. A central death registry would allow election authorities to check multiple registrations.

State officials such as secretaries of state should also be granted investigative subpoena powers to look into both vote fraud and disenfranchisement issues. Historically, election offi-cials have relied too heavily on candidates to identify election problems. Most election boards do not have the authority to con-duct vigorous investigations of fraud and must rely on local dis-trict attorney's offices that are usually heavily engaged in criminal cases and not interested in prosecuting election fraud for fear of being labeled partisan or racially motivated. Election officials should have the investigative powers necessary to pursue cases and to impose administrative fines on violators. Similarly, state attorneys general should be authorized to use statewide grand juries to investigate election fraud anywhere in a state.

Local registration and election boards should be composed of citizen appointees. All such boards should have equal representation from both major political parties and at least one independent or third-party member. We've seen over and over, from St. Louis to Palm Beach County, how conflicts of interest are created if election boards are run by officials who have to run for offices themselves—often as partisans. "I think you'll see most of the problems in bad management of elections occur where the top position isn't nonpartisan and where most of the oversight is by people deeply involved in the political process," says Mischelle Townsend, former registrar of voters in Riverside County, California.

All county and municipal election authorities should be required to have independent audits conducted of their vote tabulation systems, software and security procedures on a regular basis. In business, companies undergo outside audits by independent bodies to confirm to their stockholders that the companies are truthfully reporting on their financial condition and status. Election bodies should also be required to have outside audits to confirm to their stockholders, the voting public, that their security procedures are sufficient to guarantee free and fair elections.

Independent, nonpartisan groups, as well as candidates and parties, should be authorized to appoint poll watchers to observe the election and the vote tabulation. Poll watchers are essential for running elections that are free of fraud and manipulation. In addition to having poll watchers in specific precincts, parties and candidates as well as nonpartisan groups should be able to designate statewide poll watchers with authority to observe activities at any precinct or vote tabulation center.

All vendors who supply voting machines and computer software should be required to undergo investigation for financial solvency, security and integrity. Most states have no such requirement for election vendors. Only an investigation similar to the one that lottery vendors must undergo in most states can ensure that manufacturers of election machines have a good track record in other jurisdictions and won't manipulate voting results.

Decisions on which ballot-counting technologies to use should remain at the state and local level. However, we should phase out "central counting stations" where punch-card, touch-screen or optical-scan ballots are tabulated, often requiring the ballots to be moved from one location to another before being counted. Far more spoiled ballots turn up at these central stations than at individual polling sites, because voters cannot be notified of their errors on site.

We should take seriously concerns about poor election administration in racial minority neighborhoods. Even though the claims by the U.S. Commission on Civil Rights that there were conscious attempts to intimidate minority voters in Florida in 2000 were baseless, the commission did identify concerns that many minority voters have about the system. These have been bolstered by recent polls showing that some one out of seven minority voters don't believe their ballots are counted correctly. At the same time, we should not let charges of racism distract us from the push for reform. A study by two political scientists, Martha Kropf and Steven Knack, found that African Americans live disproportionately in counties with *more* reliable voting technology. Antiquated equipment is largely located in counties with white and Republican majorities.

Clear and consistent rules for identifying what constitutes a vote and for the timetables and procedures for contesting an election result must be developed by each state. Disputes over the vagueness in Florida's election law inflamed the controversial 2000 recount. The Supreme Court in *Bush v. Gore* held that voters in states should be given "equal protection of the law" in assuring that all votes are counted equally, but also held that its ruling wouldn't be a precedent in other cases. Establishing the legitimacy of a vote is a tricky business. Overvotes, for two or more candidates, and undervotes, for no candidate, can have very different meanings. Overvotes are usually the result of a mistake, but about 70 percent of undervotes are deliberate because a voter didn't want to make a choice.

Honoring Our Troops

The federal government should undertake to ensure that states handle military ballots in a fair and expedited manner. As E. J. Dionne of the *Washington Post* put it, "Absentee ballots from service members overseas need to be treated with the utmost care and subjected to ballot-counting criteria that are, at a minimum, no more stringent than those applied to regular ballots."

The problem is real. Samuel Wright of the National Defense Committee, a pro-veterans group, says he has counted 7,838 different state and local election offices that administer federal elections and communicate with troops overseas. A substantial minority, perhaps 40 percent or more, of military personnel who try to vote by submitting completed Federal Post Card Applications are unable to do so because of overly complicated absentee voting procedures and, most importantly, inadequate ballot transmission time. (Military personnel almost always use the FPCA to apply for absentee ballots because this federal form is available from military voting assistance officers and because federal law requires all states to accept the form.)

In 2003, Missouri's secretary of state, Matt Blunt, sent a questionnaire to local officials asking for a report on how military ballots are handled. Blunt, who is now Missouri's governor, had a real interest in the issue as a lieutenant commander in the Naval Reserve. After 9/11, he was recalled to active duty and sent outside the United States for several months—the only statewide elected official so called to active duty.

Secretary Blunt distributed the questionnaire to Missouri's 116 local election officials and received responses from 105 of them. (The City of St. Louis was one of the holdouts.) Those 105 election officials reported receiving 1,147 completed postcard applications for ballots in the 2002 general election. No doubt some ballots were sent out and not returned; we will never know that number. We do know that only 673 of those applicants (58.7 percent) ended up casting ballots that were counted. Clearly, many other ballots were either lost or disqualified—a situation we should remedy.

The problem is that most states are still conducting absentee voting essentially as they did in World War II, depending upon snail mail for all three steps: the transmission of the absentee ballot request from the voter to the election official, the transmission of the unmarked ballot from the election official to the voter, and the transmission of the marked ballot from the voter to the election official. Each of these steps can take weeks if the mail must be used, but only seconds if secure electronic means were authorized.

In 2006, a bipartisan group of twelve senators—five Democrats and seven Republicans—wrote to the Pentagon asking for the creation of a new voting system that would allow soldiers to easily "request, receive, download and print" absentee ballots regardless of their location. So far, the Pentagon's response has been slow and halting. Nothing much has changed since it abandoned a pilot electronic voting program in 2004 due to cost overruns and bureaucratic snafus.

I favor a simplified system that is two-thirds electronic: the service member should be able to make an electronic application for an absentee ballot, and the election official should be able to transmit the unmarked ballot to the military voter by electronic means. Then, the voter could print out the ballot and the required affidavit and return envelope. Until we have greater confidence in the technology, we should require all absentee voters to return their marked ballots by U.S. mail or a commercial delivery service like DHL or FedEx. At least one of these companies is interested in carrying military ballots under a contract that would charge a pittance of the normal shipping charges.

The Road Ahead

Many Americans still smart from a history of discriminatory hurdles to voting, and they instinctively resist anything that smacks of exclusion. That is understandable. We should oppose any attempt to create artificial barriers to voter participation.

Discrimination can take many forms: turning away voters already in line when polls close, intimidating or misinforming voters when they arrive at the polls, using badly flawed or poorly designed ballots, failing to provide bilingual materials, failing to fix problem voting machines. We must guard against all these practices. But we also must recognize that voters have responsibilities to acquaint themselves with the election process and they cannot expect that their vote will be counted no matter what mistakes they make in casting it. Better voter education in schools, literacy programs, and public service announcements before an election, reminding people what they must do to cast a valid vote, can all help reduce the number of spoiled ballots and ensure that as many valid votes as possible are cast.

We also should consider paying the people who run our elections more, as well as giving some of them more professional training. We pay many of the election officials in some of our rural counties less than the janitors at the local school. Sue Woody, who had served as the clerk of Park County, Indiana, resigned last year because she couldn't make it on her salary of $22,000. She was responsible for running both the court and the election systems for her county.

But we also have to return to the traditional view that citizenship requires orderly, clear and vigorous procedures to ensure that the integrity of our elections is maintained. An era of rampant egalitarianism has influenced the election process to the point where opportunists or enthusiasts can take advantage of casual "inclusive" rules to alter the course of public affairs. "The more rules are settled in advance, the better elections we will have," says Brad King, a former state elections director of Minnesota, who is now co-director of Indiana's elections division. "What we don't want is the designed sloppiness that a few politicians allow to seep into our system through ambiguity and vagueness." Ambiguity in election law is a surefire recipe for funny business at the polls, litigation afterward, and a chance that some votes won't be counted properly.

But few in the media or urban governments seem concerned about the designed sloppiness of our election system. There is also an increasing brazenness by many people who want their side to cut corners if it helps them win. Michael Moore is free to put out *Fahrenheit 9/11* in a direct attempt to defeat George W. Bush, but he is not supposed to use his celebrity status to make light of influencing people to vote. In the "Do Something" section of his website he suggests that supporters of John Kerry "offer a six-pack to anyone in the office who votes (make sure you've not working in cubicles full of Republicans!) ... Promise to have sex with a non-voter—whatever it takes!"

Our current lax enforcement of voting laws, in which prosecutors shy away from bringing election fraud cases unless the evidence is almost literally handed to them on videotape, is analogous to having counterfeit bills circulating and the Treasury not wanting to be bothered until the printing press is located.

Should "anything goes" continue to be the ballot byword, the nation may wake to another crisis even bigger than the 2000 Florida folly. Perhaps then it will demand to know who subverted the safeguards in its election laws. But wouldn't it be better if—with the lessons of Florida and even more recent election snafus and scandals still fresh in the minds of many people—we did something now?

Acknowledgments

E XPRESSING APPRECIATION TO THOSE WHO HELPED MAKE A
book possible is always a tricky endeavor. You are
almost certain to forget someone, so apologies are
offered in advance to anyone whom I inadvertently pass over.

This book would never have been possible if I didn't have
the opportunity to work at the editorial page of the *Wall Street
Journal*, the most congenial and supportive workplace imagi-
nable for someone who wants to examine and comment on
issues of the day. Paul Gigot, the editor of the editorial page,
knows a good story when he sees so much of the media ignoring something. He allowed me to spend a great deal of time on
the topic. James Taranto, Howard Dickman and Robert Pol-
lock vastly improved many of the articles I wrote for the *Journal*. Steve Moore and Brendan Miniter, two other *Journal*
colleagues, were valuable sounding boards. Some sections of
this book are drawn in part from material previously published
in the *Wall Street Journal* and its website.

I am especially grateful to Roger Kimball and Peter Collier
of Encounter Books for believing in this project. Encounter's
staff pulled off amazing feats of speed and vigor in bringing
this book to you, the reader, before the 2008 election. I appreciate the help of Carol Staswick for copyediting and for making all the pieces fit just so. The book also benefited from
Heather Ohle and all the other wonderful people at

Encounter. Martin Wooster stepped in to do some critical research; any author would benefit from his meticulous combing of libraries.

I am in debt to those in the think tank and philanthropic world who provided helpful advice, including John Samples of the Cato Institute, Ed Feulner of the Heritage Foundation, Brian Anderson and Myron Magnet of the Manhattan Institute.

Many chapters were improved by conversations with Brenda Burns, Darcy Olsen, Linda Morrison, Gay and Stanley Gaines, Dan Walters, Grover Norquist, Gail Heriot, Heather and James Higgins, Mallory Factor and Jon Caldera. I will always be grateful to Clara del Villar for her encouragement.

Democrats such as Paul Goldman, former Virginia governor Doug Wilder, the late congressman Ned Pattison, Karen Saranita, Melody Rose and former Philadelphia city councilman James Tayoun offered indispensable help in separating serious voting problems from partisan complaints. Martha Montelongo, Leon Louw of South Africa and Tunku Varadarajan provided me with perspectives on voting and ballot security from outside my culture. I owe my father more than I can ever say; and although my mother passed away just as I was finishing this book, I am happy that she was able to read most of it in draft form.

Notes

Introduction

page 2 A Rasmussen Reports survey—Survey of 800 likely voters, January 2–3, 2008.

2 Congressional Cooperative Election Studies— Stephen Ansolabehere and Nathaniel Persily, "Vote Fraud in the Eye of the Beholder: The Role of Public Opinion in the Challenge to Voter Identification Requirements," *Harvard Law Review*, 2008.

5 John Kerry campaigned in Florida—FOX News transcript, April 19, 2004.

5 Barack Obama has been even more forceful—*Chicago Defender*, October 8, 2007.

7 This system was instrumental—Interview with President Vicente Fox, March 11, 2001.

9 The late Earl Mazo—Peter Baker, *Washington Post*, November 11, 2000.

11 The U.S. attorney for the Northern District of Louisiana—*Shreveport Times*, August 31, 2003.

Chapter One: A Conflict of Visions

13 Zogby found that 9 percent—*Houston Chronicle*, July 9, 2000.

13–14 "Then one of the workers brought out ..."—Interview with John Zogby, July 9, 2004.

15 On the other side of the aisle—Letter posted on web-site of Democratic National Committee's Voting Rights Institute, July 2, 2004.

18 But the city attorney, Louise Renne—Interview on KCBS Radio, July 10, 2004.

18 Meanwhile, many Republicans I met carried a brochure—Florida Department of Law Enforcement Report on Voter Fraud, January 1998.

19 According to the pollster Scott Rasmussen—Interview with Scott Rasmussen, June 1, 2008.

20 "If I erred in doing so ..."—*Indian Country Today*, November 4, 2002.

20 Donna Brazile, who served as Al Gore's campaign manager—Interview with Donna Brazile, September 10, 2003.

22 The subject remains a sensitive one—Interview with David Keene, June 9, 2004.

23–24 the North Carolina Republican Party mailed—Interview with Donna Brazile, September 10, 2003.

26 Horrocks had contempt for Allen—Interview with Francis Allen, May 11, 2004.

28 Gans believes that the deadwood—Interview with Curtis Gans, July 8, 2004.

31 In a 2003 study—Christopher Uggen and Jeff Manza, "Felon Disenfranchisement: Law, History, Policy and Politics," *Fordham Urban Law Journal*, September 2005.

32–33 Elizabeth Hull, a professor at Rutgers University—Elizabeth Hull, "Disenfranchising Ex-Felons: What's the Point?" *Social Policy*, March 2003.

Chapter Two: Voters without Borders

36 "Washington State has regressed ..."—Interview with John Carlson, February 2, 2008.

39 Elizabeth Drew quotes Bill Clinton—Elizabeth Drew, *Whatever It Takes: The Real Struggle for Political Power in America* (Viking Press, 1997).

41 "They represent an invitation …"—Interview with Robert Pastor, September 15, 2006.

43 She says it hasn't raised turnout—Interview with Melody Rose, August 3, 2002.

Chapter Three: From Little Oaks Grows a Mighty Acorn

48 "I have one lady, I have five applications on her"— *New York Times*, June 15, 2008.

51 The King County prosecutor—*Seattle Post-Intelligencer*, July 27, 2007.

51 "It's a potential recipe for fraud"—Interview with Melody Powell, November 1, 2006.

52 "We met twice with ACORN …" —Interview with Matt Potter, October 31, 2006.

52 Rathke told me—Interview with Wade Rathke, November 2, 2006.

53 "The internal motto is …"—Interview with Nate Toler, October 17, 2006.

53 Barton alleges that—Interview with Loretta Barton, October 18, 2006.

Chapter Four: Barack Obama and ACORN

57 He called his book "a step toward …"— Saul Alinsky, *Rules for Radicals*, reissued edition (Vintage Books, 1999).

58 Hillary Clinton met three times—Scott M. Kershner, "Speed-Hump Victory," *Christian Century*, May 20, 2008.

60 Obama became ACORN's attorney—Abdon M. Pallasch, *Chicago Sun-Times*, December 17, 2007.

60 Obama was effusive in his praise—Sam Graham-Felsen's Blog, incorporated into Obama '08 campaign website, February 21, 2008.

60 While Jerry Kellman of ACORN—*Foundation Watch*, Capital Research Center, June 2008.

61 ACORN also runs something called—*Chicago Sun-Times*, September 4, 2007.

62 This prompted Senator Palmer—CNN Newsroom, May 30, 2008.

Chapter Five: The Battle for Photo ID

67 The dangers and threats—Jingle Davis, *Atlanta Journal-Constitution*, November 6, 2000.

69 The department relied on statistics—Letter from William E. Moschella, U.S. Department of Justice, to Senator Chris Bond, October 7, 2005.

69 In fact, Senator Barack Obama—*Chicago Defender*, October 8, 2007.

72 "[W]e need to find one or more …"—E-mail from Daniel Levitas, August 8, 2007, 5:07 P.M.

74 A third witness who was deposed—Deposition of Annie L. Johnson, August 29, 2007, p. 30.

79 Georgia even had a substantial increase—Interview with Robert A. Simms, Georgia Secretary of State's Office, January 15, 2008.

84 A newspaper in Hoboken, New Jersey—*Hudson Reporter*, July 1, 2007.

85 Von Spakovsky also remarked—"Stolen Identities, Stolen Votes," Heritage Foundation, March 10, 2008.

85 On the day of the oral arguments—Cindy Bevington, *Fort Wayne Daily News*, January 9, 2008.

86 Voter ID had no negative effect—Jeffrey Milyo, "The Effects of Photographic Identification on Voter

Turnout in Indiana," University of Missouri, November 2007.

87 As Heritage pointed out—Heritage Center for Data Analysis report, September 10, 2007.

87 A similar study by professors—Jason Mycoff, Michael Wagner, and David Wilson, "The Effect of Voter Identification Laws on Aggregate and Individual Level Turnout," paper presented at the annual meeting of the American Political Science Association, August 2007.

Chapter Six: A Supreme Court Victory

92 Justice Stevens witnessed all this—Interview with Joe Morris, a longtime Chicago lawyer, February 28, 2008.

92–93 In 1987, when the high court vacated—*Chicago Tribune*, June 25, 1987.

94 Jay Stewart, the executive director—Brian Ross, ABC News.com, February 29, 2008.

Chapter Seven: The Myths of Florida Live On

98 "I've had discussions …"—Peter Kirsanow, *National Review*, July 12, 2004.

99 Lott found that among the twenty-five—U.S. Commission on Civil Rights, Minority Report, August 2001.

100 But the liberal-leaning *Palm Beach Post*—*Palm Beach Post*, May 28, 2001.

108 "They just couldn't be bothered"—Interview with John Lott, June 21, 2004.

109 But more than 3,000 voters—Interview with Theresa LePore, December 4, 2000.

Chapter Eight: Mississippi Stealing

111–12 "blacks, being the majority race ..."—Associated Press, July 1, 2007.

115 "... I'll send the police on around to arrest you."—Court opinion, Judge Tom S. Lee, U.S. District Court, Southern District of Mississippi.

116 "They come over and vote ..."—Associated Press, June 11, 2007.

Chapter Nine: The Fraud That Made Milwaukee Famous

126 Attorney General J. B. Van Hollen—Associated Press, February 27, 2008.

126 But Governor Jim Doyle—*Green Bay Press-Gazette*, March 9, 2008.

127 "By allowing people to register in person ..."—U.S. Senator Russ Feingold, press release, May 1, 2008.

Chapter Ten: Florida with Rain

130 Jason Osgood wants to make sure—*Seattle Times*, June 3, 2008.

130 Reed vociferously disagrees—Interview with Sam Reed, December 12, 2004.

132 Democrats spent the next three days—*Seattle Times*, November 14, 2004.

133 "When you're talking about close to 900,000 pieces of paper"—*Seattle Post-Intelligencer*, December 2, 2004.

133–34 "Every time you have human judgment ..."—Interview with Bruce Chapman, former Washington secretary of state, December 20, 2004.

137 Even the office of Ron Sims—*Seattle Times*, April 8, 2005.

139 There was also a precedent for a statewide rerun—Interview with Bill Gardner, New Hampshire secretary of state, September 9, 2006.

140–41 "My goal was to figure out ..."—Interview with Stefan Sharkansky, May 3, 2008.

141 When I called to ask her why—Interview with Judge Betty Fletcher, May 8, 2005.

146 Washington State's widespread use of mail-in ballots—Associated Press, April 7, 2005.

149 But he can't help but wonder—Interview with Tom McCabe, November 4, 2006.

Chapter Eleven: Politically Active after Death

151 "Hey, stay for the election. ..."—Steve Hilton, *St. Louis Post-Dispatch*, March 28, 2002.

153 Not that Judge Baker didn't have—Bill McClellan, *St. Louis Post-Dispatch*, November 12, 2000.

156 But Dowd never told Judge Baker—*Insight*, July 16, 2001.

157 Some of the orders were clearly—*St. Louis Post-Dispatch*, December 5, 2000.

159 Secretary Blunt's investigation—Missouri Secretary of State's Report on Conduct of Elections in City of St. Louis, May 2001.

161 In March 2002 he focused television network news—Interview with Senator Kit Bond, June 17, 2002.

163 On election night, Hearne and Jack Bartling—Interview with Thor Hearne, January 30, 2003.

164 McCaskill, now a U.S. senator from Missouri—Audit Report of the Missouri State Auditor, May 26, 2004.

Chapter Twelve: Vote Fraud the Old-Fashioned Way

168 After his fall from power—Mark D. Hirsch, "More Light on Boss Tweed," *Political Science Quarterly*, June 1945.

171 James Harrison, a biographer— James Harrison, *The Life and Letters of Edgar Allan Poe* (Crowell & Co., 1903).

172 The historians Gary Cox and Morgan Krause—*The Dynamics of Electoral Turnout, 1870–1980* (Praeger, 1992).

173 The Hague machine turned vote fraud—Interview with Bret Schundler, former mayor of Jersey City, October 11, 2007.

Chapter Thirteen: The Ghost of LBJ

176 They discovered men burning ballots—Interview with Kay Daly, November 13, 2000.

177 "There is a lot of abuse ..."—*San Antonio Express-News*, April 4, 2004.

178 Debra Danburg, a Houston Democrat—Glenn R. Simpson and Evan Perez, *Wall Street Journal*, December 19, 2000.

179 Gilberto Quezada, the author—*San Antonio Express-News*, April 9, 2004.

Chapter Fourteen: How to Steal an Election from Jimmy Carter

183 In response to critics, Carter called—FOX News transcript, September 19, 2005.

185 According to a Carter campaign worker—*San Francisco Chronicle*, February 14, 1993.

186 Carter recalls a 1964 debate—Jimmy Carter, *Turning Point: A Candidate, a State, and a Nation Come of Age* (Times Books, 1993).

Conclusion: Where Do We Go from Here?

187 A few years ago, Marsha decided—Interview with Warren Olney, July 14, 2004.

189 Senator Chris Dodd of Connecticut—Interview with Senator Chris Dodd, April 15, 2002.

193 In 2002, there was a thirty-five-day delay—Interview with Donetta Davidson, Colorado secretary of state, December 11, 2002.

196 Opposition to photo ID laws—*Wall Street Journal*, March 13, 1997.

197 Eye-popping examples—*Reader's Digest*, August 1997.

197–98 David Jordan, a Democratic state senator—*Jackson Clarion-Ledger*, February 20, 2004.

199 Some precincts run out of ballots—Interview with Mary Kiffmeyer, former Minnesota secretary of state, October 11, 2006.

200 "His view is that voters …"—Interview with Garry South, Gray Davis campaign adviser, November 18, 2003.

202 In 2002, trial lawyers were extremely active—*Wall Street Journal*, November 6, 2002.

205 "All of us know that absentee voting …"—Interview with Doug Lewis of the Election Center, March 6, 2007.

206 During a bitter recount—*Orange County Register*, April 20, 1997.

209 The problem is real—Interview with Captain Sam Wright, September 10, 2007.

210 Each of these steps can take weeks—Interview with Captain Flagg Youngblood, Young America's Foundation, August 1, 2006.

212 "The more rules are settled in advance ..."—Interview with Brad King, co-director of the Indiana Elections Division, July 19, 2004.

Index

Moore, Homer, 184
Moore, Michael, 96, 98, 102, 212
Moritz College of Law (Ohio
State), 87
Motor Voter Law: *See* National
Voter Registration Act
MoveOn.org, 133
Mrvan, Frank, Jr., 22–23
Munro, Ralph, 138
Murillo, Elder, 179
Murphy, Austin, 39
Murphy, Harold U., 70, 75–78
Murphy, Tom, 70

NAACP (National Association
for the Advancement of Col-
ored People): on California
recall, 19; and felon voting, 97;
on photo ID, 69, 70, 72, 80, 81,
89; on precinct voting, 191
Nance, Earl, Jr., 160
Nasaw, David, 170
National Association of State
Election Directors, 205
National Commission on Federal
Election Reform (2001), 41
National Defense Committee,
209
National Labor Relations Board,
53
National Voter Registration Act
("Motor Voter"), 6, 27–30; and
ACORN, 59; and St. Louis
fraud, 159; and turnout, 201;
and voter ID, 6
National Welfare Rights Organi-
zation, 49
Navarro, Teresa, 178

NBC, 102
Nelson, Jean Y., 157
Nevada: Las Vegas scheme, 26–27
New Hampshire, 25, 36, 197
New Jersey, 10, 24; Jersey City,
172–74
New Mexico, 194–95
New Orleans, 7, 9
New Orleans Times-Picayune, 47,
48
New York City: Tammany Hall,
167–71
New York Independent, 170
New York Morning Journal, 170
New York State, 182; Nassau
County, 9, 23; naturalization
standards, 168; noncitizen vot-
ing, 17; Utica, 13–14
New York Times: on Florida
recounts, 97, 140; on Tam-
many, 170–71
noncitizen voting, 9, 17–18, 29,
97, 206
North Carolina, 23–24; revote,
138
nursing home fraud, 15, 39–40,
145, 202

Obama, Barack, 1, 2, 5; and
ACORN, 57, 59–61, 63, 93–94;
and Alinsky, 57, 59; and
Chicago politics, 92, 93–94;
hardball tactics, 61–64; on ID
requirements, 69, 92, 93–94;
and "Motor Voter," 60, 93; and
New Mexico primary, 195
Oberkramber, Janalyn, 158
Odom, Mark, 156–57